THE BLOODSTAINED PATH TO GOD

Experiencing Worship With Old Testament Believers

Daniel and Sarah Habben

Northwestern Publishing House
Milwaukee, Wisconsin

Cover illustrations: Lars Justinen; GoodSalt, Inc.
Inside cover chart: John C. Lawrenz
Interior Illustrations: Keith Neely
Art Director: Karen Knutson
Design Team: Pamela Dunn, Lynda Williams

Northwestern Publishing House
1250 N. 113th St., Milwaukee, WI 53226-3284
www.nph.net
© 2012 by Northwestern Publishing House
Published 2012
Printed in the United States of America
ISBN 978-0-8100-2391-8

TABLE OF CONTENTS

INTRODUCTION 5

ONE
The Heart of the Torah, *Part One* 14

TWO
The Heart of the Torah, *Part Two* 22

THREE
Cleanliness Laws 37

FOUR
The Feast of Tabernacles 45

FIVE
The Tabernacle and Temple. 51

SIX
The Sabbath. 61

SEVEN
The Priesthood 68

EIGHT
The Five Sacrifices. 78

NINE
The Burnt Offering. 88

TEN
The Fellowship Offering. 97

ELEVEN
The Sin Offering. 103

TWELVE
The Guilt Offering 109

THIRTEEN
The Passover. 116

FOURTEEN
Feast of Weeks/Pentecost 125

FIFTEEN
Feast of Trumpets 133

INTRODUCTION

Purpose of this book

Good photographers understand how contrasting light and shadow enhances a composition. In a similar way, God has recorded "shadows" of Christ in the Old Testament in order for us to see the light of the Savior more clearly.

Unfortunately, many Bible readers find that those shadows of Christ leave them in the dark! As you read Leviticus, for example, rather than being enlightened, you may find yourself groping through unfamiliar details and obscure obligations. You wouldn't be the first to skip over books like Leviticus in search of more digestible material. In fact, if your church follows the three-year cycle of Bible readings included in *Christian Worship*, you will hear only one Leviticus passage every three years![1]

However, "*All* Scripture is God-breathed and is useful" (2 Timothy 3:16). God designed and recorded these Old Testament laws for a reason. If we bypass these pages of Scripture, we cheat ourselves of a deeper understanding of God's plan of salvation. This book is intended to help you navigate the Old Testament ceremonies, festivals, and laws with a sense of confidence rather than confusion—and with more than that, with a sense of wonder at God's graphic love for sinners!

The heart of the Torah

Getting to the heart of a matter means you are attempting to find its center or pulse. Present-day writers often reveal the heart of

---

[1]One additional Leviticus reading (Good Friday, Series B) has been added to the supplemental lectionary in the *Christian Worship: Supplement.*

their work only at the end. But if you were an ancient Hebrew author, you would help your readers locate the heart of your poetry or prose by plunking it right in the *middle* of the work. That's where we will look for the heart of the Old Testament laws. We will burrow into their center.

First, though, we need to understand where in the Bible the Old Testament laws are found. The simple answer is in the books of Moses. Yet *books* is not the best term to use to describe Moses' writings. God's inspired author Moses wrote only *one* book, which the Jewish people called the Torah, or Law. This one work was divided into five parts, which we call the "books" of Genesis, Exodus, Leviticus, Numbers, and Deuteronomy. Moses' single book was divided into these five parts for purely practical reasons. The book of Moses was far too long to squeeze onto the 25-foot scrolls used by the Israelites. A longer scroll wasn't the solution, since it would be too heavy to lift. Instead, the writings of Moses were divided into the five books we have today. The Greek term for Moses' writing, *Pentateuch,* or *five volumes,* is an appropriate name for this body of work.

By remembering that the Torah is really *one* book, we can more easily find its center, heart, and pulse. A simple count tells you that the third scroll, which corresponds to the book of Leviticus, lies at the center of Moses' writings. (As we go along, we will be referring to the Torah chart at the beginning of this book.)

"Hmmm, . . . " you might think, "Leviticus? But that book is so, to put it bluntly, dull!" True, compared to the thrills and chills of Genesis and Exodus, it is easy to get bogged down once your home devotions enter the chapters of Leviticus. The hundreds of commandments in the Torah seem to belong to an alien culture. All that slaying of cute and furry animals! All those suffocating lifestyle restrictions! All those complicated and curious rituals! To those of us who were weaned on action-packed Bible stories like Noah's ark and David and Goliath, it may come as a surprise that in Jesus' day, unwieldy Leviticus was the first portion of the Torah studied by Jewish children.

"Poor things!" you think. "But surely we present-day Christians have little to gain from studying those obsolete laws. Are they really the 'heart' of the matter?" The simple answer is yes! The book of Leviticus with its sin-payments, substitutes, and sacrifices is the forensic scientist's equivalent of finding multiple clear fingerprints. For the Old Testament *believers*, those fingerprints created their identity. They were like fingerprints that clearly distinguished them from the ungodly nations living next door. Their fingerprints especially identified them as heirs of God's promised forgiveness and linked them to the Savior.

By faith, we in the New Testament have those same fingerprints. They identify us as followers of the same Savior whom the Old Testament Jews looked forward to. Like the Emmaus disciples, our hearts too are "burning within us" as we become aware of the intricate, inspiring links between the Old Testament laws and their fulfillment by the Lamb of God (Luke 24:13-32).

Now burrow deeper. The central chapter of Leviticus is chapter 16. Here is the heart of the heart. What we read about in this chapter is the most important lesson God wants to teach us through his servant Moses. But what is so important about the rituals described in Leviticus chapter 16? Why would Moses draw particular attention to this part of the Law by cushioning it between all the other directives for faithful, orderly worship found in the Torah? That is where we will start in chapter 1 as we follow the bloodstained path that God directed his Old Testament people to walk. But first, a few more comments on the Law.

Thankful obedience

The multitude of Old Testament laws leads some people to conclude that the Israelites were to earn salvation by obeying the commandments. Not so. Romans 3:28 tells us that Old Testament believers were saved in the same way as New Testament believers are. Both are "justified by faith apart from observing the law." God's relationship with his people has always followed the same pattern: God *first* acts on his people's behalf, *then* he asks for their obedience. New Testament Christians understand this. While we were still sinners, Christ won our salvation. *Therefore*, we live lives of thankful obedience (Romans 5:8; 12:1). Old Testament believers understood this too. God told the Israelites at Sinai, "Although the whole earth is mine, you will be for me a kingdom of priests and a holy nation" (Exodus 19:5,6). This promotion from anonymous to anointed was surely not a reward for good behavior. The Israelites' exodus was a trail of tears and testing, of mutiny and mudslinging! No, God's blessings on Israel were acts of mercy. And the commandments? They were given *after* God had rescued them from slavery in Egypt. In grace, God chose insignificant Israel to receive his revelations, preserve his Word, and bear witness to his power. The Israelites strove to obey the laws God gave them in the Torah as a response to his grace.

It may also seem logical to conclude that in giving the endless laws and sacrifices of the Old Testament, God was playing the role of a playground bully: daily rubbing the Israelites' noses in their sins and holding them hostage to their guilt. It's easy to imagine the Israelites bent over beneath a burden of *fearful* obedience, dreading another day when they would only fail yet again to meet God's demands.

This book strives to highlight how the Old Testament laws were not only God's stern voice of judgment (law) but also his assuring voice of merciful love (gospel). That mercy shines in God's promise to the Israelites in Leviticus 16:30, where he tells his people, "Before the LORD, you will be clean from all your sins." Each sacrifice, *upheld by God's promise*, truly forgave and atoned for sins. Each sacrifice pointed the Israelites to the real payment for sin: the atoning blood of Jesus. His death on the cross would pay off every sin-debt—past, present, and future.

King David had faith in the promised Messiah. He trusted that God had a final solution to his sin. That is why he did not drag his heels en route to God's house. Instead, he set off with a spring in his step and a song of *thankful* obedience: "At his tabernacle will I sacrifice with shouts of *joy*" (Psalm 27:6). It is our hope that you will experience some of this joy as you accompany some Old Testament believers along the bloodstained path to God.

How this book is organized

This book begins with the heart of the Torah: the Day of Atonement detailed in Leviticus chapter 16. The foldout in the front cover will help you visualize the important central role this day plays in the five books of Moses.

Each chapter begins with one or more readings from Scripture that describe the laws addressed in the chapter. If you wish, spend time reading the entire section in the reference located before the short excerpt provided. The chapter then continues with background material to create a context for the laws.

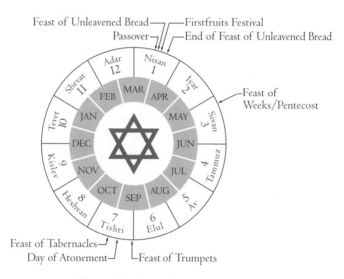

The Jewish Church Calendar

The laws are then "dramatized" within a vignette to help make God's instructions personal and to demonstrate the spirit in which God wanted his people to observe them. These little stories address the who, what, where, when, how, and why questions about the Old Testament laws and ceremonies. The Lord set up a "church year" for his Old Testament people, just as your church follows a church year, starting with Advent and Christmas and continuing through Easter and Pentecost. On this page is a chart of the Jewish church year.[2] You will see this chart at the beginning of each chapter to orient you to the season of the church the chapter describes. The details of rituals and festivals within these vignettes are either taken directly from the Bible or from long-standing Jewish tradition.

Each chapter closes with a "Sacred Silhouette," a section that briefly explains how these rituals pointed ahead to Christ and were fulfilled by him.

In the vignettes you will meet four main characters: Natan, a devout Jewish father; Shlomo, his 11-year-old son; Jeshua, a young priest new to his role; and Johanan, the high priest. Johanan is a historical figure who seems to have served as the high priest in the latter days of King Solomon's reign and the beginning of King Rehoboam's reign. He is little more than a name listed in I Chronicles 6:9, and any portrayal of him in these vignettes is fictional.

Two locales are used in the vignettes: the city of Hebron and the holy city of Jerusalem, 25 miles to the north of Hebron. The sacrifices and other rituals take place in Solomon's temple rather than in the tent-church, or tabernacle, that Moses built for the Israelites in the wilderness—although the same laws were followed in both places.

A little historical background

The vignettes are set in 930 B.C., shortly after King Solomon's death. Although Solomon strayed from God's Word when he married scores of wives and was ensnared by their idol worship (I Kings 11), his reign was a highpoint in Israel's history. It was a time when, for the most part, God's temple was revered, his priests served faithfully, and the people were devoted to God's laws.

---

[2]We will use the present-day Jewish calendar, in effect since the Babylonian captivity. The month names vary somewhat from those referenced in Scripture. For example, in Scripture the first month is called *Abib*, but in the present-day calendar, it is called *Nisan*.

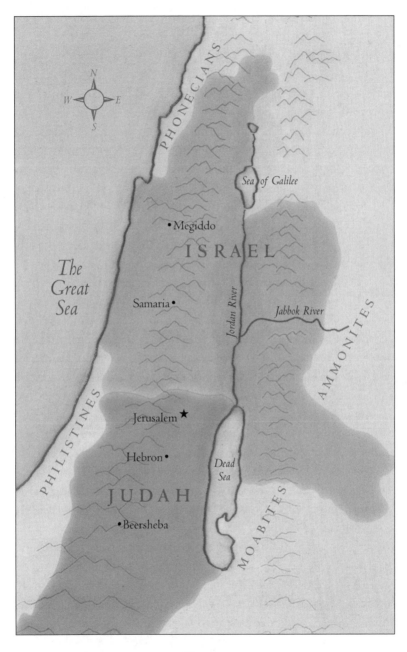

Canaan

After Solomon's death, the kingdom split into two parts—Judah in the south and Israel in the north. Solomon's son Rehoboam became king in Judah at age 41 and reigned for 17 years. For the first three years of his kingship, he was "walking in the ways of David and Solomon" (2 Chronicles 11:17). During those years King Rehoboam fortified cities along major roads, including Hebron, putting his sons in charge of them and filling the cities with military commanders and stores of food and weapons (2 Chronicles 11:5-12,23). King Rehoboam also received the faithful priests and Levites who were expelled from the Northern Kingdom of Israel by the unblushingly wicked King Jeroboam, who had gleefully set up non-Levite priests to minister before false idols in the shapes of goats and calves (2 Chronicles 11:15). People from the Northern Kingdom "who [had] set their hearts on seeking the LORD, the God of Israel" were also welcomed in Judah, where they fled so they could continue worshiping the true God (2 Chronicles 11:16).

The vignettes in this book are set within this three-year period. They describe the various laws, offerings, and pilgrimages as if the majority of Jews still observed them. In reality, the system was a broken one. Rarely does the Bible record even major festivals being observed, and then only in a belated attempt to resurrect them. Second Chronicles chapters 29 and 30 tell the fascinating history of King Hezekiah's spiritual reforms. He began his reign by reopening the temple, which by his day had been abandoned (715 B.C.). You can almost hear the rusty doors screeching open and see Hezekiah's men shredding cobwebs as they walked through the Holy Place. Then Hezekiah had to round up the negligent priests and Levites for a stern lecture! Under Hezekiah's direction, both the temple and the hearts of the Levites underwent a renovation in time for a Passover celebration, the likes of which hadn't been seen since Solomon's reign. Nehemiah 8:9-18 provides another example of a spiritual revival (445 B.C.).

The regrettable mouthful of forbidden fruit Adam and Eve ate in the Garden of Eden means that people can no longer walk as friends with God, let alone stay in step with his holy expectations. Our sins, like those sins of old, have built a chasm between us and a holy God. But God has bridged the chasm! God began building the bridge with the Old Testament system of sacrifice, which provided a blood covering for the Israelites' sin and foreshadowed the superior sacrifice of God's Son, Jesus.

It's time to set our feet on that ancient, bloodstained path to God. Our journey through the Old Testament laws will begin on the Day of Atonement, in the month of *Tishri*, the seventh month in the Jewish calendar year. This month, because of all the sacred festivals found in it, is the most holy month in the Jewish church year. It is a signpost on God's path that points directly to the cross and the cleansing blood of Christ.

THE HEART OF THE TORAH,
PART ONE

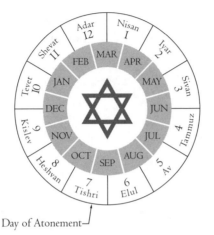

Day of Atonement

Bible reading

Leviticus 10 and 16—Nadab and Abihu's Disobedience

Aaron's sons Nadab and Abihu took their censers, put fire in them and added incense; and they offered unauthorized fire before the LORD, contrary to his command. So fire came out from the presence of the LORD and consumed them, and they died before the LORD. Then Moses said to Aaron and his sons Eleazar and Ithamar, "Do not let your hair become unkempt, and do not tear your clothes, or you will die and the LORD will be angry with the whole community. But your relatives, all the house of Israel, may mourn for those the LORD has destroyed by fire." (Leviticus 10:1,2,6)

The LORD spoke to Moses after the death of the two sons of Aaron who died when they approached the LORD. The LORD said to Moses: "Tell your brother Aaron not to come whenever he chooses into the Most Holy Place behind the curtain in front of the atonement cover on the ark, or else he will die, because I appear in the cloud over the atonement cover.

"This is how Aaron is to enter the sanctuary area: with a young bull for a sin offering and a ram for a burnt offering. He is to put on the sacred linen tunic, with linen undergarments next to his body; he is to tie the linen sash around him and put on the linen turban. These are sacred garments; so he must bathe himself with water before he puts them on." (Leviticus 16:1-4)

Leviticus chapter 16 is not only the heart of the Torah, it has also been called the drama of our salvation. It describes the Day of Atonement rituals that, according to God's promise, (1) cleansed the people of all their sin and (2) cleansed the sanctuary from all impurity. God intended this annual salvation drama to cause his people to long for the promised Messiah, who would do for them what was being enacted symbolically.[3]

Leviticus chapter 16 opens with a flashback to the fiery fate of Aaron's unpriestly sons, Nadab and Abihu. These men, who had just been ordained into the priesthood, offered incense to God in a manner that dishonored the Lord (Leviticus 10:1-3). In response, God struck them dead with fire. Because Aaron was the high priest, he was not allowed to touch a dead body, so he had to squash his natural impulse as a parent to touch the bodies of his sons or even mourn their sudden death. Instead, he kept a silent vigil in the tabernacle, replaying in his mind God's object lesson: no one may dare approach God on their own terms because God is holy and human beings are not. This was troubling for Aaron. After all, his own prints were all over a previous crime scene where he had hosted an idolatrous party with a golden calf as the guest of honor. His weakness had led to the death of three thousand Israelites (Exodus 32). How could he ever stand in God's holy presence and survive?

In Leviticus chapter 16, God teaches Aaron the proper way to approach him so that Aaron would not be destroyed. God shows Aaron how to decontaminate himself—not with bleach, but with blood. With blood Aaron was to cleanse himself, the sanctuary, and the community from "all the wickedness and rebellion of the

---

[3] Armin J. Panning, *Romans*, of The People's Bible series (Milwaukee: Northwestern Publishing House, 2001), p. 62.

Israelites—all their sins" (Leviticus 16:21). This included uninten-tional sins of which the priest or community was unaware.

This head-to-toe cleansing was scheduled for once a year on the Day of Atonement, a day that made a polluted people "at one" with a holy God. The Hebrew term for the Day of Atonement is *Yom Kippur.* The basic word in this term could be translated as either "day of covering," "day of removing," or "day of ransom." Although these translations seem unrelated, they all draw an accurate picture of the rituals of Yom Kippur. On this day the Israelites' sinful fin-gerprints, so offensive to their holy God, were *covered* by the blood of substitute animals. Their sinful deeds were *removed* onto the back of a scapegoat. And all this was possible because of the future *ransom* Jesus would pay with his blood.

The majority of the yearly rituals and ceremonies were con-ducted with the help of an entire division of priests and Levites. However, the duties of Yom Kippur belonged almost exclusively to the high priest. As you will soon see, it was a day that demanded of the high priest a mind for detail, the arm of a butcher, plenty of footwork, and, most important, a heart of repentance.

Our vignette in this chapter opens soon after the civil new year celebration, the first day of the month *Tishri.* Like us, the Jews cele-brated a civil year (which for us is celebrated on January 1) and a church year (which for us begins at the end of November). The first month of the Israelite civil year was *Tishri,* and the first month of their church year was *Abib,* or *Nisan.* As you can see from the church year diagram, the great Day of Atonement figured prominently into both the civil year and the church year. (*Tishri* is in the fall of the year, and *Nisan [Abib]* is in the spring.)

In the vignette you will meet an 11-year-old boy named Shlomo and his father, Natan. They live in the town of Hebron, 25 miles south of Jerusalem. Observe the feelings of this Jewish family as the tenth day of *Tishri,* the Day of Atonement, approaches—emotions perhaps similar to those of a present-day Christian who looks forward to receiving Holy Communion after a long absence. As a devout Jewish father, Natan is following God's command in Leviticus 16:29 to participate in the Day of Atone-ment by resting and fasting.

The story—Natan prepares his family for the Day of Atonement

The ninth day of *Tishri* drew to a close under a pregnant gray sky, following months of dry summer heat. The crops were long stored, the fruits gathered, and the land was awaiting the autumn rains. Shlomo's father, Natan, turned from the doorway and clapped his hands together, sending out a small puff of dust.

"Yes, Shlomo, my son, if Yahweh[4] wills, we will soon have rain! So God softens the ground for the new crop. It is a good time to study the Torah. So God softens our hard hearts with his Word."

Shlomo grinned. It was a speech he had heard every *Tishri* since he was born, 11 seasons ago. His Aba loved to study and discuss the words God had given Moses, and none were more dear to him than the vivid details and instructions of Leviticus.

Natan continued his annual speech. "Tomorrow is the tenth day of *Tishri*, the great Day of Atonement. We will rest from our work and deny our bellies. We will mourn over our sins that separate us from God.

"But," Natan smacked his breast, "we also have hope in our hearts, Shlomo! For tomorrow the Most Holy Place will be open to the high priest. Blood will be dashed on God's mercy seat! Our sins will trot off into the desert on the scapegoat! Our guilt will be lifted, and the sanctuary will be cleansed! That, Shlomo, is God's gracious promise to us."

Aba's hands settled on Shlomo's shoulders with a painful squeeze. "Come. Sit down with your old Aba. Let us begin our review in the heart of the Torah, with Yom Kippur, the Day of Atonement."

On cue, Shlomo asked his father, "Why do you call the Day of Atonement the *heart* of the Torah, Aba?"

"It is in the heart of the Torah that we see God's heart for sinners. You and I cannot stand before a holy God unless our sins are

---

[4]Jewish tradition states that God's name, often written as *Yahweh*, was only spoken by the high priest on the Day of Atonement (Mishnah Yoma 6:2). Otherwise the people addressed God as *Adonai* (my Lord), *Ha-Shem* (the Name), or simply *Elohim* (God). Since it's not clear when this practice started, our vignette characters will use the more familiar *Yahweh*.

covered. God designed the rituals of the Day of Atonement to do just that. Because of his promises, God hides his face from our sins and blots out all our guilty deeds" (Psalm 51:9).

"But we perform sin and burnt offerings all year long, Aba. What makes Yom Kippur different?"

"Hmmm." Natan scrubbed rapidly at his beard with one thick forefinger as he considered an explanation. "Think of your mother. You know your Ima loves you because she tells you so. Despite your great, long legs, she allows you on her lap! She keeps you clean. She rises early every morning to bake your bread. But every now and then she throws into that dough a handful of sweet raisins. Why does she do this? Every mouthful you chew of that raisin bread is saying, 'I love you.' Ima is telling you in a new way that you are her dear son."

Natan ignored the audible growl from Shlomo's empty stomach. He flung out his arms, a wide smile creasing his leathery face. "So much does God cherish Israel that on the Day of Atonement he assures us in a fresh, new way that we are forgiven and our offerings are accepted. He paints us a picture that we cannot ignore: all the sins that weigh on our hearts are confessed over the scapegoat, who carries them out of sight, as far as the east is from the west! And not only are God's people cleansed, but also his temple! Just think, Shlomo, all year our sins have darkened the doorways of God's house. They have soiled his sanctuary and are piled in a stinking heap on his altar. Just as we do not allow our own oxen to stay in a filthy stall, how much less can we expect God to dwell in the midst of our sin? Those sins must be hauled out! True, the high priest won't use a pitchfork to remove those sins. He'll use the lifeblood of a bull and a goat. I don't know how it all works, Shlomo, but that's what God promises. And when all is purified, God's people can approach his altar again and meet with him there."

"And yet, Aba, we are never done being cleansed, for the Day of Atonement comes every year."

Natan regarded him solemnly. "You are right, son. God in his mercy leaves our sins unpunished. But for perfect, permanent cleansing we must wait for the Promised One, who will crush Satan and redeem God's people."

A smile pleated the corners of his eyes. "Now, call your sister and mother. We will begin our review of the heart of the Torah, so we can see in here"—he tapped his head—"and here"—he tapped his heart—"what is about to take place on our behalf in Jerusalem."

Sacred silhouettes

How many of these Old Testament laws and rituals were properly understood as road signs pointing to the Savior? Devout Jews searched the laws and rituals for any connection to the first promise of a Savior (Genesis 3:15). There God had promised that someone born of a woman would "crush" Satan. And he himself would be "struck" in the process.

No doubt the Israelites understood that their sacrifices were connected with the promised Savior, whom they referred to as the Messiah. They understood that *their own* blood should have been shed and *their own* bodies burned on the altar of burnt offering as just punishment for sin. Instead, the laws of sacrifice made it clear that God would accept a lamb in their place as punishment for the sins of each and every one of them!

As time went on, God added details to the pictures he had painted in Leviticus. Already in Deuteronomy 18:15-19 Moses directed the Israelites to look forward to the Great Prophet whom God would raise up from their nation—a fellow Jew, a human being, just like one of them. Later, prophets like Isaiah and Micah added more pieces to the puzzle, specific details about the Messiah's birth and death. (For some good examples, stop and read Isaiah 7:14; 9:6,7; all of Isaiah chapter 53; and Micah 5:2.)

It may seem to us that the details of God's plan of intervention were rather sketchy. Yet the Holy Spirit delivered flashes of insight to believers like Job, who could make the startlingly precise confession: "I know that my Redeemer lives" (Job 19:25). How many other such flashes of insight went unrecorded during the long years of anticipation? Perhaps more than we can imagine.

It is a great tragedy that despite the Old Testament "road signs," the priests and other religious leaders of Jesus' day allowed the Old

Testament shadows of the Messiah to *overshadow* the living, breathing reality—the Messiah himself, Jesus of Nazareth! He was the fulfillment of generations of bloody preliminaries. Just as the paparazzi today make it their business to spot a star, even dressed incognito, so the Jewish religious leaders should have stampeded to Jesus the Messiah when his words and actions matched the Old Testament prophecies they knew so well. Indeed, Jesus himself said, "You diligently study the Scriptures because you think that by them you possess eternal life. These are the Scriptures that testify about me, yet you refuse to come to me to have life" (John 5:39,40).

The Old Testament testimony to the Messiah came not only in the form of direct prophecies of what he would do but in a myriad of pictures and in a grand performance in which the Israelites themselves were actors. The yearly, monthly, and daily scheme of sacrificing forced God's people to think about the aspect of life that he considered most important—the forgiveness of sins.

Perhaps you have already begun to wonder what these sacrifices actually achieved. You might especially wonder about the apparent contradiction between God's promise in Leviticus 16:30b, "Before the LORD, you will be clean from all your sins," and in Hebrews, where the writer states that the annual sacrifices were only a "reminder" to the people of their sins "because it is impossible for the blood of bulls and goats to take away sins" (Hebrews 10:3,4).

So which was it? Did the sacrifices only highlight sin and remind the Israelites of their guilt, or did they truly cover sin over and give forgiveness? Look at it this way. Each sacrifice *highlighted* sin by forcing Old Testament believers to constantly confess that their sins were serious and deserved the death penalty. The animal sacrifices, however, were not themselves the payment. They were essentially I.O.U. notes from God. In one sense every sacrifice was a promise from God, that he himself would someday offer a sacrifice which would have real and lasting value. In mercy, God left the sins of his people unpunished, having planned from eternity to punish his own, sinless Son instead (Romans 3:25).

At the same time, the sacrifices truly covered sin and gave forgiveness to Old Testament believers. On its own the blood of these animals couldn't actually do anything. But the blood was used by God's command and connected with God's Word. God attached a promise to those sacrifices; a promise that linked the people to the atoning blood of Jesus.

Does this remind you of our New Testament Sacrament of Baptism? Baptism saves because plain water, which is powerless on its own, is used by God's command and with his word of promise. While Baptism looks back on Jesus' sacrifice for forgiveness, the Old Testament sacrifices looked ahead to it. To be beneficial, both rites require faith, which God alone gives.

Although God's people had to wait for the Messiah, God did not make them wait for forgiveness or peace. His system of animal sacrifice, upheld by his promise, not only drove home their need for a Savior but also gave them real rest and freedom from their burden of guilt. Truly cleansed. Truly forgiven. No wonder relief resonates in King David's words: "When we were overwhelmed by sins, you forgave our transgressions" (Psalm 65:3). Old Testament believers did not find a wrathful, terrifying God at the altar of burnt offering; they met the Savior-God.

THE HEART OF THE TORAH,
PART TWO

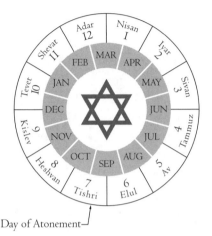

Day of Atonement ⌐

Bible reading

Leviticus 16—The Day of Atonement

> *Aaron is to offer the bull for his own sin offering to make atonement*
> *for himself and his household. Then he is to take the two goats and*
> *present them before the LORD at the entrance to the Tent of Meeting.*
> *He is to cast lots for the two goats—one lot for the LORD and the*
> *other for the scapegoat. Aaron shall bring the goat whose lot falls to*
> *the LORD and sacrifice it for a sin offering. But the goat chosen by*
> *lot as the scapegoat shall be presented alive before the LORD to be used*
> *for making atonement by sending it into the desert as a scapegoat.*
> *(Leviticus 16:6-10)*

To a present-day Christian, Leviticus chapter 16 is a mind-
bending mayhem of animals, bloodletting, and the high priest's
back and forth trips through the sanctuary. You might reach the
end of the chapter and wonder, "What just happened?"

It may help to think of the Day of Atonement as a play with
three acts:

Leviticus 16:1-19—Act I: The temple is cleansed with the blood of the sin offerings.

Leviticus 16:20-22—Act II: Sin is removed in the scapegoat ritual.

Leviticus 16:23-25—Act III: Israel is rededicated to God with the burnt offering.

ACT I

Wearing a simple, white garment, the high priest cleanses the sanctuary from the inside out, moving from the Most Holy Place, out to the Holy Place, and then into the courtyard where the altar of burnt offering is located. Later, he incinerates the fat of the bull and goat for the sin offering on the altar. All remains—innards, hide, flesh—are carried outside the temple precinct to be burned.

ACT II

The sins of the Israelites are transferred to a goat, which is led away into the desert and, according to Jewish tradition, thrown backward off a cliff so that there is no danger of their sins somehow returning to the camp.

ACT III

Having completed the atonement rituals, the high priest changes from his white linen garments into his royal garments and offers one ram as a burnt offering for himself and a second ram as a burnt offering for the people.

Here's a synopsis of this sacred drama:

Among the characters, the high priest is the most prominent. He confesses, sacrifices, sprinkles, burns, and changes his "costume."

Various animals, bulls and goats, play supporting roles. Their blood is shed to cleanse the high priest, the sanctuary and its furniture, and the people. One of these animal characters is the unlikely "scapegoat," a goat chosen by lot to carry the sins of the Israelites into the desert. Some translations use the Hebrew term *Azazel* for the scapegoat, which is commonly translated as "(e)scapegoat" or "a departing goat." In modern Hebrew, the words *lekh la-azazel* are the equivalent of the English "go to hell," which is precisely where the Israelites wanted their sins to go!

Two other men play supporting roles. One is the man in charge of leading away the scapegoat. Another is the man who carries the remains of the animals "outside the camp" to be burned.

The "audience" of Israelites plays a part: by resting and fasting. Interestingly, this was the only annual fast God commanded in the Old Testament.

The offerings made on the Day of Atonement not only atone for the sins of the people but have an added purpose. They cleanse the sanctuary, which throughout the year has been soiled by the people's sins. On this day, and only on this day, the blood is carried into the Most Holy Place and sprinkled on the cover of the ark of the covenant, referred to in the NIV translation as the "atonement cover" (Leviticus 16:13).

There is a lot of activity on the Day of Atonement. To help us envision the back and forth movement of the high priest and where the sacrifices are being carried out, it will be helpful to have diagrams of Moses' tabernacle and Solomon's temple in mind. Solomon's temple is where our stories unfold. The following brief explanations will help you understand the terms that occur in Leviticus chapter 16 and in the accompanying vignette.

The Tent of Meeting. This structure had two rooms, the Holy Place and the Most Holy Place. Only priests could enter the Holy Place, and they did so twice daily to offer incense. Only the high priest could enter the Most Holy Place. He did so only once a year, on the Day of Atonement. The original Tent of Meeting was a little larger than a big motor home (45 x 15 feet) and

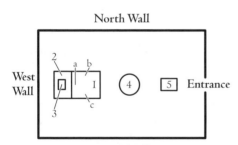

North Wall

West Wall

South Wall

1. The Holy Place
   a. The Altar of Incense
   b. The Table of Showbread
   c. The Lampstand
2. The Most Holy Place
3. The Ark of the Covenant
4. The Bronze Basin
5. The Altar of Sacrifice

Tabernacle

held in place by 95-pound silver bases. The frame was covered in four different layers of fabric and animal skin that were secured by bronze pegs. Solomon's temple was larger in size. It was made with stone, paneled with cedar, and covered with gold on the inside.

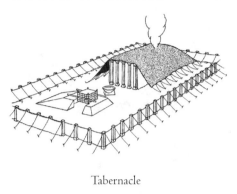

Tabernacle

Entrance to the Tent of Meeting. This term refers to the eastern courtyard of the tabernacle, in front of the altar of burnt offering. The entrance area may have extended from the altar to the courtyard entryway. This same term may also refer simply to the main entrance into the tabernacle compound, the curtains at the east end that could be pulled back to allow entry. (See Leviticus 8:3,4 and 9:5.)

In tabernacle times, the entire courtyard was less than half the size of a football field (150 x 75 feet). Posts hung with white linen marked its boundaries. Only those who were ceremonially clean could gather in this zone to interact with the Lord and present their offerings. (It may have been the case that only Levites could enter the tabernacle courtyard, but this is not entirely certain.)

King Solomon designed a stone and cedar wall of unknown height at the far end of the courtyard of his temple, restricting access to the temple and the altar of burnt offering. This wall separated the "large court" (where ceremonially clean worshipers from all the tribes of Israel gathered) from the "courtyard of the priests" (which only Levites could enter). (See 2 Chronicles 4:9.)

Atonement Cover. Inside the Most Holy Place was an object known as the ark of the covenant. It was a box that held the Ten Commandments. The top of the box was known as the mercy seat, or atonement cover. It was sometimes called the footstool of God's throne (1 Chronicles 28:2). This was a flat cover made of pure gold that was fixed to the top of the ark of the covenant. On either end of this cover was an angel made of gold. Between these

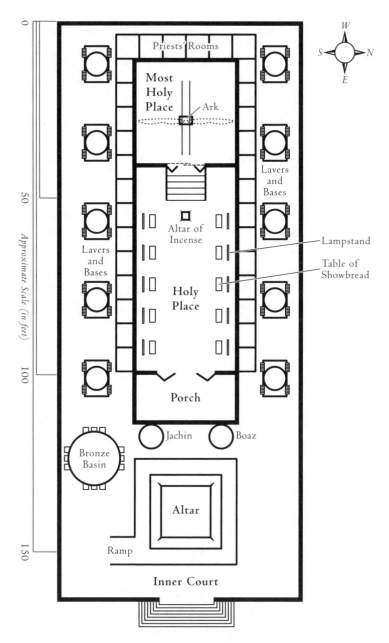

Solomon's Temple

two angels, called cherubim, God appeared in a cloud to meet and speak with Moses. On the Day of Atonement, the high priest entered the Most Holy Place to sprinkle blood on and in front of the atonement cover.

Altar of Burnt Offering. This altar stood in the outer court. It was where God met with his people when they presented sacrifices and offerings, where their sins were atoned for, and where they received God's blessing (think of Aaron raising his hands to bless the people at the end of his ordination in Leviticus 9:22). It was also a place of refuge (Solomon's brother, Adonijah, sought asylum at the horns of the altar in I Kings I:50 after a failed attempt to usurp the throne of Israel). The original altar was 7.5 feet square and 4.5 feet high (envision two large dining room tables arranged side by side). It looked like a hollow box that stood on a grate.

Ark of the Covenant

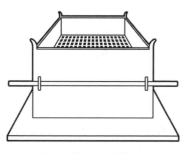

Altar of Burnt Offering

The altar in Solomon's temple was about the height of a present-day two-story house, 15 feet high and 30 feet wide. The priests used a ramp to bring the offerings to the top of the altar. Its tabletop surface was large enough for three woodpiles: one for offerings, one for incense coals, and one for the perpetual fire (ignited personally by God on Aaron's ordination day, and then ignited by God again at the dedication of Solomon's temple).

Despite its looming size, the altar was never intended to give the Israelites the idea that they were going up to God. Rather, it was the means by which God reached down to them and interacted with them on earth, even as he promised in Exodus 20:24: "I will *come to you* and bless you." (More on the arrangement of and articles in

Priest Offering a Sacrifice

Solomon's temple can be found in I Kings chapter 6 and in the introduction to Vignette 5.)

High Priest's Garments

The Priest's Uniform. Exodus chapter 28 describes the priest's wardrobe, as designed by God. It also explains why the uniform was to be worn: to give dignity to Aaron and his sons and to keep them from being destroyed when they served God in the tabernacle. The high priest's usual regalia (which included a golden diadem) was taken off on the Day of Atonement and replaced with simple, white linen garments. This may have illustrated his transition from an envoy of the King of kings to serving as a representative of a sinful people. More detail on this uniform will be provided in the upcoming vignette.

In the next vignette, you will accompany the high priest Johanan on Yom Kippur, the Day of Atonement. Though Johanan has enacted the rites of this significant day many times before, they still inspire in him great awe and wonder.

The story—The high priest Johanan prepares for the Day of Atonement

I.

The high priest Johanan was lost for the moment in thoughts of the past. He was remembering the last days of his father, who had served as high priest during the reign of King Solomon. Johanan had watched at his father's bedside until it became evident that he would not recover. According to the Law of Moses, being in the presence of death made one unclean. As the next high priest, Johanan could not defile himself even for a beloved family member. On his last visit, however, he had bent over the sickbed and pressed his father's limp hand to his lips, willing himself not to blink and spill the tears that trembled behind his eyelids.

His father's lips moved slowly. Johanan bent so low that his father's breath whispered on his cheek. He recognized the words of King David: "And I—in righteousness I will see your face; when I awake, I will be satisfied with seeing your likeness" (Psalm 17:15).

"When you awake . . ." Johanan's throat clenched as he finished his father's sentence. "When you awake, you will be satisfied with seeing God's likeness."

The ghost of a smile crossed his father's lips. As Johanan backed out of his father's room for the last time, he imagined his father awaking in heaven and seeing God, no longer walking with trembling steps through the smoke of incense but face-to-face.

Soon after his father died, Johanan was ordained as high priest in place of his father. Senior priests washed Johanan from head to foot and then helped him slip into a woven white tunic and a blue robe hemmed in purple and scarlet yarn. The small golden bells stitched to the robe tinkled softly as the priests tied his sash. Arms outstretched, Johanan waited while they secured the blue, scarlet, and gold ephod on his shoulders with its two onyx stones, each engraved with the names of six of Israel's tribes.

"You will bear the names of the sons of Israel as a memorial before the Lord."

Two priests lifted a heavy breastplate over Johanan's head and settled it on his shoulders. Its four rows of precious stones glinted dully in the dim light of the chamber. One priest murmured, "Whenever you enter the Holy Place, you will bear the names of the sons of Israel over your heart." Johanan lowered his head so they could place the turban on him. Its gold plate was engraved with the words, "HOLY TO THE LORD." For the rest of his life he would bear the guilt of the Israelites as their mediator before God (Exodus 28:38).

Years had passed since Johanan had been anointed and ordained high priest, and now he was no young man himself. He stood beneath the altar of burnt offering in the eastern courtyard of the temple, his robes glowing in the late afternoon light. He was aware of the weight of the ephod on his shoulders, the weight of the nation he carried. In the morning, on the Day of Atonement, his richly hued robes would be exchanged for plain, white linens, and he would approach the mercy seat of the King of kings as a servant and representative of a sinful nation. He whispered, "Who am I to stand before God? Wash me with hyssop, Lord. Cleanse my iniquity. Circumcise my heart."

Behind him someone cleared his throat. Johanan turned to see an elderly priest, who inclined his gray head in greeting.

"Shalom, Elior."

"Shalom. The sacrificial animals are ready for your inspection. Once you have approved them, the elders will lead you a final time through the order of the Atonement rituals so your preparation for tomorrow is complete."

A clatter of hooves followed this announcement, and a group of Levites and priests led in Johanan's sin offering, a young black bull. It was closely followed by two goats, placidly chewing their cuds, blissfully unaware that in a few hours one goat would be sacrificed as the nation's sin offering and the other would be driven into the desert carrying an invisible burden of sin. Two rams joined the train of animals for inspection. These would be sacrificed as burnt offerings for Johanan and the nation.

Johanan and the priests slowly walked the line of animals, running their hands across twitching flanks, lifting ears, inspecting eyes, searching for any defects or blemishes. Animals that were blind, injured, or marred by boils or scabs could not be presented to the Lord.

The animals passed inspection and were led away to chambers to await the morning. Johanan paused before following the elders into the outer rooms to continue his final preparations for Yom Kippur. He stood a moment in the courtyard, the vast bulk of the altar of burnt offering looming behind him. This is where God met his people and blessed them. Tomorrow he would follow the Lord's directives to cleanse the sanctuary and purify the nation so that the sons and daughters of Israel could approach their holy God safely at his altar.

II.

Johanan rose before daybreak and bathed. He drew on his sacred white linen undergarments, tunic, sash, and turban, aware of the absence of the reassuring weight of the ephod and breastplate. He contemplated the enormity of the task that lay ahead of him. Not for the first time his thoughts turned to Aaron, that first high priest. It was Aaron who had led the Israelites into idolatry right under God's nose. Aaron who had silently witnessed the deaths of his sons, fellow priests, at the hands of a just God. Aaron who was then invited to approach God's mercy seat on behalf of the mutinous millions who wandered in sin along with him. How must he have felt? Johanan thought he knew. Inadequate. Unworthy. Yet privileged beyond compare. Under his breath he sang the words of King David's psalm: "Blessed is he whose transgressions are forgiven, whose sins are covered" (Psalm 32:1). Today was Yom Kippur—the Day of Covering. Blessed indeed were sinners like him.

Johanan assumed his special place in the procession that wound through the temple courtyard. Flanked by his assisting priests, Johanan passed through the cool shadow cast by the two great bronze pillars of the temple portico and descended the stairs into the courtyard. The young bull stood impassively near the immense stone altar. Johanan first had to sacrifice this animal for his own sins before he could approach God on behalf of the people. He drew near the bull and pressed his two hands on its head, between its horns. Only the bull's moist, dark flank moved, twitching away the flies that had already gathered in the morning heat. Johanan confessed for himself and his family in a strong, clear voice: "O Lord, I have sinned against you, I and my household. I beseech you, O Lord, grant atonement for the sins we have committed against you. Remember your words to your servant Moses, that on this day atonement shall be made for us to purify us from all our sins."[5]

Johanan then turned toward the two goats tethered in front of the altar. Their ears flicked forward, and they scrutinized him with their strange, yellow eyes. Anticipation shivered through the watching crowd. It was time to choose the scapegoat. A wooden lottery box was brought to Johanan. He thrust in both his hands. Quickly he withdrew the two lots that lay inside. The lot in his right hand was inscribed with the words, "For the Lord." He fastened the lot to the goat on his right. It would be a sin offering to the Lord. The lot in his left hand was for the scapegoat. Johanan fastened the lot to the second goat, turning the animal to face the eastern gate through which it would later be led into the desert, carrying its burden of sin.

Johanan was now ready to slaughter the bull for his personal sin offering. The bull's head was fastened to a ring, and Johanan swiftly tugged the knife across its outstretched neck, catching the blood of his offering in a vessel. Warm, sticky blood spattered his bare feet and darkened the hem and sleeves of his white robe. When he had begun his priesthood years ago, his stomach had twisted at this sudden, hot spilling of life. Now Johanan felt no disgust. Without the shedding of blood there was no forgiveness. He handed the full vessel to a fellow priest, who rotated it gently so the blood wouldn't congeal.

Necks craned to watch Johanan climb up the center of the wide ramp that led to the top of the altar of burnt offering. He carried a golden shovel that he thrust into the fire, sending up a swirl of smoke and embers. He pulled it out, filled with burning coals, and carried the shovel down the ramp. Another priest brought him a container

[5]Alfred Edersheim, *The Temple* (Grand Rapids: Eerdmans, 1972), p. 310.

of finely ground incense and an empty ladle. Johanan scooped up two handfuls of the powdery incense and carefully poured it into the ladle. Holding the shovelful of coals in one hand and the ladle of incense in the other, Johanan crossed the courtyard and climbed the steps that led into the temple.

Before him were the golden doors to the Holy Place. He stepped inside. The air that spilled from the closed room was cool and perfumed by incense, ashes, and greasy tendrils of smoke. Bars of light slanted across the floor from windows near the ceiling, but it was the flickering light of ten lampstands that made the golden walls of the Holy Place seem to ripple. Their flames quivered as Johanan walked past them toward a second set of doors. Behind these doors hung a thick curtain whose blue, purple, and crimson folds were embroidered with cherubim. Beyond the curtain hid the Holy of Holies. There Johanan would stand before God's mercy seat in the holiest place on earth. Johanan's bloodstained hands gripped the coals and incense. His heart hammered in his ears. He drew a deep breath and stepped into the Holy of Holies.

The sight that greeted him once a year filled his heart with awe. In the dim light two great, golden angels, 15 feet tall, stood against the back wall of the Most Holy Place, their wings outspread. The outer wing of each angel touched the walls on either side, and their inner wings met at the tips in the middle of the room. Beneath these impressive sentries was the ark of the covenant. Johanan knew that inside the ark were the two stone tablets bearing the Ten Commandments.

The atonement cover of the ark was topped by two smaller cherubim, one on each end. Long, golden poles extended from either side of the ark, which Levite hands had once grasped to carry the ark during Israel's 40 years in the desert.

Johanan took in the scene through lowered eyes. The Law of Moses directed the high priest to burn incense in the Most Holy Place. The cloud of smoke would hide from his eyes the mercy seat—the place where God dwelled—so that he would not die. Johanan placed his shovel of coals between the two poles of the ark. With immense care he tipped the incense from the ladle into his hands. Johanan sifted the two palmfuls of incense onto the glowing coals in the shovel. A fine residue clung to his sticky hands. Then flames jumped up from the coals, and soon the entire chamber was dense with the smoke of his incense offering. Johanan backed reverently out of the Most Holy Place, paused to pray, and then retraced his steps through the Holy Place, across the temple porch, and down the stairs into the courtyard.

His reappearance raised an audible sigh of relief from those waiting outside. He had safely emerged from the presence of God. Johanan took the blood-filled vessel from the hands of the assisting priest and returned to the Most Holy Place, this time holding the blood of his sin offering. Smoke swirled around Johanan as he stood between the poles of the ark and dipped his finger into the vessel of blood. With his forefinger, he sprinkled the blood on the cover of the ark and then seven times in front of the ark. Again, he backed out of the Most Holy Place and returned to the courtyard.

With a scrape of hoof on stone, the goat that had been designated "For the Lord" was led to Johanan. He sacrificed the animal, catching its blood in another vessel. This was Israel's sin offering. For a third time Johanan climbed the stairs into the sanctuary and entered the hazy gloom of the Most Holy Place. Standing between the poles of the ark, he sprinkled the blood with his forefinger, just as before. With relief, with reluctance, he backed out of God's presence a final time. Safely on the other side, he sprinkled the blood of the bull and the goat in front of the entryway to the Most Holy Place.

Johanan turned to the altar of incense in the Holy Place, on which incense was burned every morning and evening. The Law of Moses said to "make atonement on its horns" once a year. Again he dipped his finger into the two vessels of blood, smearing each of the small altar's four horns. With these symbolic acts, atonement was made for the sanctuary, for himself, and for all Israel. Then Johanan returned to the courtyard. One final act of atonement remained, for the altar of burnt offering.

Johanan poured one vessel of blood into the other until the blood of the bull and the goat were thoroughly mixed, and then he ascended the altar ramp. He strode from one corner of the altar to the other, daubing the four horns of the altar with blood and sprinkling the surface with blood seven times. Now the altar of burnt offering was purified from the sins of the people. God could again come to his people and bless them there.

Johanan approached the scapegoat, the sin-carrier. With all his strength he pressed his hands against the animal's knobbly head. It bleated its protest and then fell silent. For a moment Johanan was still, aware only of his bloodstained fingers against the whorl of fur on the goat's head. Then he shut his eyes and began to pray for the entire nation of Israel, confessing aloud all their wickedness, rebellion, and sin, pressing their sins onto the goat's head. When he was done, a man stepped forward and led the bleating scapegoat out of the courtyard and through the East Gate. Every head turned to follow its departure. Every ear strained to trace its passage down the mount by the shouts of Israelites along the path: "Take our sins and go! Go!"

Though he was physically drained, a great burden seemed to lift from Johanan's shoulders. He hurried into the temple side rooms to immerse himself in another ritual bath. He changed from his linen garments into his priestly regalia, again the ambassador of the King.

He returned to the courtyard, his robes a vibrant splash of color, and concluded the rituals of the Day of Atonement by sacrificing the two rams as burnt offerings, rededicating himself and the people to the Lord. To the flames he added the fat of the sin offerings— the bull and the goat—and watched as the oily smoke spiraled into the air, its sweet smell drawn into the nostrils of a merciful God.

Sacred silhouettes

The author of a mystery novel plants evidence in the first chapters that will lead from crisis to resolution. Invariably, the novel presents a victim, a motive, and hopefully, a dose of justice. The story of humanity begins with a crisis in the Garden of Eden. God, the Author of Life, already knows how the crisis will be resolved. He begins a systematic planting of "evidence," beginning with the clues found in the promises of Genesis 3:15. All the evidence in the Old Testament points, with increasing clarity, to the New Testament resolution: the cross. At the cross we find the motive for Jesus' suffering: God's anger with sinners . . . and God's love for sinners. At the cross, in a cliff-hanger twist, Jesus goes from victim to victor. At the cross Satan and death are disarmed. On the cross the crisis of sin is finally, thrillingly, solved.

Some 1,500 years before Jesus took on human flesh, God gave Israel the Day of Atonement, a dramatic ceremony that anticipated Jesus' work on the cross. Of all the Old Testament evidence of Christ and his redemptive work, the rituals of the Day of Atonement are among the most compelling. The New Testament points to this evidence to show that Jesus is our High Priest. Jesus' body is the curtain through which we pass into the presence of God in the Most Holy Place of heaven (Hebrews 10:20). Jesus' blood is our atonement sacrifice. And Jesus is the scapegoat who became sin for us (2 Corinthians 5:21) and then carried our sin to the cross.

Let's take a closer look at Hebrews chapter 10. The writer explains what the great High Priest, Jesus, did for us: "Day after day every priest stands and performs his religious duties; again and again he offers the same sacrifices, which can never take away sins. But when this priest had offered for all time one sacrifice for sins, he sat down at the right hand of God" (Hebrews 10:11,12). The Old Testament Day of Atonement was a temporary fix. The New Testament Day of Atonement, Good Friday, was permanent. And unlike the Old Testament priests whose job was never done, Jesus could enter God's presence and never leave. "It is finished!" he said, and with that he put an end to all Old Testament sacrificing.

The writer applies this to us: "We have confidence to enter the Most Holy Place by the blood of Jesus" (Hebrews 10:19). Johanan's hesitating entrance into the Most Holy Place is replaced with the confidence we have to step boldly into heaven. We do not need a high priest to approach God on our behalf. We access God's mercy and help every time we kneel at the altar for Communion and every time a fellow believer, on God's behalf, forgives our sins. Jesus' blood has paid our way home. Just as the Israelites took part in the Day of Atonement by fasting and resting, so we New Testament Christians participate in God's eternal Day of Atonement by remembering that we are sinful people who can rest in God's promises and live in the forgiveness Christ won for us.

Bible reading

Leviticus 11–15—God's Cleanliness Manual

The LORD said to Moses and Aaron, "Say to the Israelites: 'Of all the animals that live on land, these are the ones you may eat: You may eat any animal that has a split hoof completely divided and that chews the cud.

"'There are some that only chew the cud or only have a split hoof, but you must not eat them. The camel, though it chews the cud, does not have a split hoof; it is ceremonially unclean for you. The coney, though it chews the cud, does not have a split hoof; it is unclean for you. The rabbit, though it chews the cud, does not have a split hoof; it is unclean for you. And the pig, though it has a split hoof completely divided, does not chew the cud; it is unclean for you. You must not eat their meat or touch their carcasses; they are unclean for you.'" (Leviticus 11:1-8)

Numbers 19—Water of Cleansing

The LORD said to Moses and Aaron: "This is a requirement of the law that the LORD has commanded: Tell the Israelites to bring you a red heifer without defect or blemish and that has never been under a yoke. Give it to Eleazar the priest; it is to be taken outside the camp and slaughtered in his presence. Then Eleazar the priest is to take some of its blood on his finger and sprinkle it seven times toward the front of the Tent of Meeting. While he watches, the heifer is to be burned— its hide, flesh, blood and offal. The priest is to take some cedar wood, hyssop and scarlet wool and throw them onto the burning heifer. After that, the priest must wash his clothes and bathe himself with water. He may then come into the camp, but he will be ceremonially unclean till evening. The man who burns it must also wash his clothes and bathe with water, and he too will be unclean till evening.

"A man who is clean shall gather up the ashes of the heifer and put them in a ceremonially clean place outside the camp. They shall be kept

by the Israelite community for use in the water of cleansing; it is for purification from sin. The man who gathers up the ashes of the heifer must also wash his clothes, and he too will be unclean till evening. This will be a lasting ordinance both for the Israelites and for the aliens living among them." (Numbers 19:1-10)

The blood of goats and bulls and the ashes of a heifer sprinkled on those who are ceremonially unclean sanctify them so that they are outwardly clean. How much more, then, will the blood of Christ . . . cleanse our consciences from acts that lead to death, so that we may serve the living God! (Hebrews 9:13,14)

Some people must wear a special medical bracelet identifying their condition. The bracelet alerts others to their condition, and, like it or not, it constantly reminds the wearers that they are not completely healthy. God made his people, the Israelites, wear a kind of bracelet—his laws. The laws identified them—as people who belonged to God. But, like it or not, his laws constantly reminded them that they were not spiritually healthy.

One aspect of God's laws was detailed instructions on what God considered "clean" and "unclean." Being unclean was not a physical state, like having grimy fingernails. It was "ritual," or "ceremonial," uncleanness. People did not have to commit a sin to become unclean. They became unclean simply by touching or being affected in some way by an object or a condition God said was unclean. An Israelite could not approach God in an unclean state. *This* would make them guilty of sin.

The many ways of becoming unclean served to remind the Israelites that they lived in a fallen world and that all was not right between them and God. It was important that their uncleanness was kept as far away from the center of holiness as possible. Leviticus chapters 11–15 instructed God's people on what was clean and unclean, and it gave the priests instructions on how to enable a person to become clean again. A summary of each of the chapters in this section will show some causes of uncleanness—which could come from sources both outside and inside the body.

Animals (Leviticus 11). This chapter is an intricate list of clean animals. Included were those that chew their cud *and* have split hooves. This would include many present-day farm animals. Among the unclean animals were certain bugs, rabbits, pigs, dogs, cats, rats, and birds of prey. There are many theories as to why God designated certain animals as unclean, for example, for dietary reasons. But God doesn't tell us his reasons. One thing is certain: observing these dietary laws kept God's people separate from the pagans around them.

Childbirth (Leviticus 12). This chapter imposes a quarantine on women made unclean by childbirth. It is not the birth itself that made the women unclean but the discharges that followed (just as women were unclean during menstruation). After a designated period of seclusion (40 days after birthing a boy, 80 days for a girl), the mothers became ritually clean by offering a burnt offering and a sin offering.

Skin conditions and mildew (Leviticus 13). This chapter teaches priests how to *diagnose* skin conditions and mildew, both of which symbolize sin and death. Anyone diagnosed with an infectious disease that made him or her unclean was isolated from the sanctuary, family, and community.

Purification rites (Leviticus 14). This chapter describes the necessary rituals priests must follow in order to purify someone whose skin disease cleared up and to deal with houses infected with fungus, which made them unclean.

Bodily discharges (Leviticus 15). Any kind of genital discharge, whether abnormal (such as that caused by sickness) or normal (such as semen and menstrual blood), made a person unclean.

Even God's gift of sexual intercourse made a husband and wife temporarily unclean (but remember, this did not imply that it was sinful). One obvious reason for this was to reshape the attitudes of the Israelites toward their bodies and sexuality. This was important given the peer pressure they experienced from their pagan neighbors. Many pagans regarded blood and semen as supernatural substances and engaged in sexual intercourse as part of their worship rituals. God's classification of these emissions as unclean helped prevent his people from imitating these pagan practices.

In this chapter God also teaches his people how to purify themselves, whether by bathing, or laundering, or presenting certain sacrifices.

Death (Numbers 19). This chapter provides a remedy for the uncleanness caused by death. Death had entered the world in the Garden of Eden. Death was an intruder into God's perfect plan, and as such it was unclean. Any Israelite who touched a dead body, bone, or human grave was unclean for seven days. Even being in the home of a person who had died made one unclean. And anyone or anything touched by the unclean person was likewise unclean.

In Numbers chapter 19 God provides a remedy for uncleanness caused by death. He provides a recipe for what is called the water of cleansing. A red heifer was to be slaughtered and incinerated along with some cedar wood, hyssop,[6] and scarlet wool. The result was a special mixture of ash, which, when mixed with water, could be sprinkled on someone "for purification from sin" (Numbers 19:9). A mass use of the water of cleansing is recorded in Numbers 31:19-24, after the Israelite army battled the Midianites. Contact with death made the whole army ceremonially unclean.

It's hard enough reading about the laws of cleanness; imagine living by them! God was training his people to daily examine what went into and came out of their bodies and to ask themselves, "What does *God's Word* tell me to do?" Becoming unclean was inevitable and unavoidable. It certainly caused the Israelites to long for the Day of Atonement and especially for the Messiah, who would crush sin and Satan beneath his heel.

The story—Celebrating the Feast of Tabernacles

It is *Tishri*, the holy seventh month. The Day of Atonement has just passed, and soon all devout Israelites will make a pilgrimage to Jerusalem for the Feast of Tabernacles.

At the sound of his mother's shriek, Shlomo paused in his shaking of the goatskin flask that hung from the courtyard fig tree. He shoved it into his little sister Miriam's hands. "Just like I showed you, Miriam. Keep shaking the milk until it curdles; Ima wants *leban* with

---

[6]We don't know the exact identity of the biblical hyssop plant. It seems to be a shrub of some sort.

dinner tonight." He ran to where his mother stood in the doorway of their home. She was holding a clay jar at arm's length. Her cheeks were an uncharacteristic shade of red.

"Another jar spoiled! As if there isn't enough to do the week before the feast!"

Shlomo took the jar and peered inside. A large, dead spider bobbed in the water at the bottom of the container, its limp legs trailing like a hem come undone.

"Please take it to the pile, Shlomo. *And don't run!*" said Ima, waggling a warning finger before vanishing into the house.

Mindful of his mother's specific warning, Shlomo didn't run. He jogged to the far corner of their courtyard, where there was a small hill of clay shards. Halfway there, he braced and flung the jar. It spun in the air, followed by a whiplash of water, and then shattered with a dull clunk against the pile of other defiled earthenware. Shlomo grinned with satisfaction. Then his eyes widened. Just inches from his feet lay the sodden spider carcass. He instinctively cranked his head to look back at the house. No Ima in sight. Shlomo breathed a sigh of relief. If that spider had touched him, he would have had to wash his clothes and been unclean until evening. Ima would not have been pleased with the extra work he had caused!

His mother was preparing for the pilgrim festival of *Sukkot*, the Feast of Tabernacles. This year Shlomo, his sister Miriam, and his mother and father would travel to the Holy City of Jerusalem to celebrate the weeklong festival. The 25-mile journey north from the hill country of Hebron to Jerusalem commenced in the morning, and Ima was more shrill than usual as she prepared food and supplies for their journey.

"And your father is only recently cleansed from burying his own poor Aba, your grandfather!" Ima cast her eyes upwards and prayed aloud, her habit when under pressure. "Lord, help us to do all that is necessary so that we can make our pilgrimage as pure people!"

The crisis having passed, Shlomo returned to the shade of the fig tree where Miriam was dutifully agitating the flask of milk.

"Another dead bug?" she queried.

Shlomo nodded, managing not to roll his eyes. "Another bug."

Bugs were a daily nuisance but, according to their Aba, such things were good reminders that all was not right between God and his people. Indeed, Shlomo knew that the Torah had dizzying lists of circumstances, from insects to mildew, that made God's people unclean. It was a sin to present oneself to God at the temple in an unclean state. Being unclean over and over again, Aba had told them, was a reminder that they drew near to God only as sorrowful sinners who wanted cleansing from their sin.

"If God did not send us spiders, how quickly we humans would forget that we are soiled goods!" Natan would say, coaxing a smile from his wife.

Natan had recently buried his own Aba. Handling the dead body of his father made Natan unclean for seven days, according to the Law of Moses. On the third and seventh days of that week, Natan had presented himself to a young priest named Jeshua, who served in Hebron. Jeshua had dipped a branch of hyssop in water mixed with the ashes of a red heifer and gently flicked it on Natan. Shlomo and Miriam had peppered their damp father with so many questions about this water of cleansing that he finally recited to them the details from the Torah, checking off the points on his stout fingers: "A rare red heifer without defect or blemish must be slaughtered and burned with cedar wood, hyssop, and scarlet wool. The ashes are kept for use in the water of cleansing, to purify from sin. Some of those ashes are placed in a jar, and fresh water is poured over them. Then hyssop is dipped in the water and sprinkled on the ceremonially unclean person or house."

On the seventh day, Natan had been purified. He had to wash his clothes and bathe with water before being declared clean that evening.

Wiggling his fingers through the wet tangles of his father's beard, Shlomo asked, "But why should you have to be cleansed just for burying your Aba?"

Natan chided him. "Remember, Shlomo, God did not plan for death in his perfect world! Death is the result of sin. When Adam and Eve rebelled, everything was affected: their relationship, their food, their bodies. When I buried your grandfather and touched his body, I had on my hands the final consequence of sin: death. If I would march into God's temple with death on my hands, I would defile his sanctuary and should be cut off from the community. But God be praised, he has given us a recipe for cleansing! Remember King David's words, 'Cleanse me with hyssop, and I will be clean; wash me, and I will be whiter than snow' (Psalm 51:7). Because of God's promise, just a few sprinkles of this special water—so! and so!—have cleansed me so that I can worship again in God's house."

Shlomo and Miriam nodded, satisfied with this explanation. Just as God had designed, the daily rhythms of life and death were awakening in them an awareness of the sinful conditions and consequences of their fallen race and deepening their longing for a Savior.

Sacred silhouettes

Even if we would stop there, one thing already stands out: the laws God gave his people were all-encompassing. We contemporary Christians might hear ourselves say, with no little pride, "My faith is the most important *part* of my life." But God did not permit his people to compartmentalize their lives. There was no saying, "This part of my life is personal, this part is work-related, and this part is spiritual." No, all of life—from birth to death, from the bedroom to the harvest fields—was to be lived under God. It was *all* spiritual! This is the very same attitude Saint Paul encourages us to embrace in I Corinthians 10:31, where we are told, "Whether you eat or drink or *whatever* you do, do it all for the glory of God."

An interesting side note to the uncleanness chapters is the Jewish practice of whitewashing all burial areas and gravestones to prevent accidental uncleanness. In Matthew 23:27 Jesus says the Pharisees are like "whitewashed tombs." Outwardly, they appeared clean. Inwardly, they were spiritually rotting corpses. That's some pretty strong imagery regarding the danger of false prophets and their infectious doctrine!

Hebrews 9:13,14 is a New Testament comment on the water of cleansing and its fulfillment by Christ. It states, "The blood of goats and bulls and the *ashes of a heifer* sprinkled on those who are ceremonially unclean sanctify them so that they are outwardly clean. How

43

much more, then, will the blood of Christ . . . cleanse our consciences from acts that lead to death, so that we may serve the living God!"

Although the New Testament does not make any further comments on the red heifer, it is interesting to consider the following parallels: Just as a red heifer was rare (Jewish tradition says there have only been nine red heifers since the time of Moses!), so Jesus is rare, one of a kind, actually. Although rare, the ashes of a red heifer were easily "stretched." Jewish tradition says that ashes from the time of the temple's destruction in A.D. 70 lasted three hundred years! Likewise, Jesus' blood is able to "stretch" and forgive all people. A mere sprinkle of the water of cleansing was enough to outwardly purify an individual, just as, more wonderfully, a sprinkle of baptismal water cleanses us from sin. Finally, just like the water of cleansing, the water of Baptism gives us life through the death of a substitute—not a red heifer, but Jesus himself.

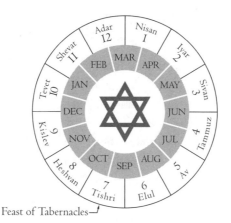

Feast of Tabernacles

Bible reading

Celebrate the Feast of Tabernacles for seven days after you have gathered the produce of your threshing floor and your winepress. Be joyful at your Feast—you, your sons and daughters, your menservants and maidservants, and the Levites, the aliens, the fatherless and the widows who live in your towns. For seven days celebrate the Feast to the LORD your God at the place the LORD will choose. For the LORD your God will bless you in all your harvest and in all the work of your hands, and your joy will be complete.

Three times a year all your men must appear before the LORD your God at the place he will choose: at the Feast of Unleavened Bread, the Feast of Weeks and the Feast of Tabernacles. No man should appear before the LORD empty-handed: Each of you must bring a gift in proportion to the way the LORD your God has blessed you. (Deuteronomy 16:13-17)

Leviticus 23:33-36—The Feast of Tabernacles
Numbers 29:12-40—Details on the Sacrifices to Be Made at the Feast of Tabernacles

As a king summons the royal officials to his palace, three times a year God summoned the heads of each Israelite household for an audience with him at his temple in Jerusalem. These three times were Passover, the Feast of Weeks (the Feast of Harvest), and the Feast of Tabernacles. No man was to come empty-handed but was to bring a gift in proportion to how God had blessed him (Deuteronomy 16:17). Devout Israelites recognized God as the owner of their land. They depended on him for their crops. They were accountable to give him their offerings. But unlike a regular king's vassals, they were actually invited to eat at God's table as privileged guests!

The first such pilgrimage followed close on the heels of the solemn Day of Atonement. It was the flamboyant Feast of Tabernacles, or Feast of Booths, beginning on *Tishri* 15. This was a festival of thanksgiving to God, who had rescued his people from Egypt's tyranny and protected them throughout four decades of strenuous, itinerant living in the desert. In a mild echo of that difficult time of testing, God required the Israelites to travel to Jerusalem and spend a week in makeshift shelters, or booths, so that "descendents will know that I had the Israelites live in booths when I brought them out of Egypt" (Leviticus 23:43).

This festival was also known as the Feast of Ingathering (Exodus 23:16). Similar to our Thanksgiving celebration, it was held at the culmination of the summer and fall harvest. God commanded his people to be joyful at the feast and gave them the reason for their joy: "The LORD your God will bless you in all your harvest and in all the work of your hands, and your joy will be complete" (Deuteronomy 16:15).

Most pilgrims arrived the day before the feast and set up their booths. According to traditional Jewish guidelines, these shelters were to be made of branches, stalks, or reeds and have at least three walls and a roof. However, there was no air of permanence about them: in fact, they were to be open to the autumn rains and the light of the stars.

A blast of trumpets in the early evening announced the start of the feast. On each of the seven days of the feast, the Israelites paraded up the temple mount and stood before the altar of burnt offering, shaking bouquets of branches called *lulavs*. With music and song they rejoiced in God's gifts and God's presence among his people.

Numbers chapter 29 describes the explosion of sacrifices and freewill offerings that also took place during the seven-day period. To handle the festive offerings over the course of the week, all 24 divisions of the priesthood were on duty.

King Solomon built the temple, which was where Shlomo and his family celebrated the feast each year. When the imposing structure finally had been completed, Solomon arranged for the ark of the covenant to be carried into its new home. The temple dedication had been held back-to-back with the Feast of Tabernacles, resulting in a two-week-long celebration. Israelites had traveled from as far as the Egyptian border, and tens of thousands of animals were sacrificed— so many that they did not fit on the altar and had to be offered up on a specially consecrated section of the courtyard (I Kings 8). For all who attended, the elation they felt at this event must have remained with them for the rest of their lives.

The story—Shlomo and his family celebrate the Feast of Tabernacles

Shlomo forgot his throbbing feet and let out an involuntary whoop of amazement as he and his family entered the Holy City. As far as his eyes could see, motley makeshift shelters sprouted from the rooftops, courtyards, gardens, and streets of Jerusalem. Some shelters were no more than loosely connected branches; others looked like they were still growing: with leaves and vines and even dripping ripe clusters of fruit. Shlomo peered into the open shelters that lined the street and could see families reclining on rugs within, mothers tying together palm and willow branches for *lulavs*, fathers and grandfathers giving a firm shake to this or that post to test its steadiness, children tumbling in and out of their neighbors' shelters.

It was *Tishri* 14, the day before the Feast of Tabernacles. Just four days earlier, the Day of Atonement had been solemnly observed by all Israel as a day of rest and repentance. But the sorrow and reflection of that pivotal day was now cast off by God's command to "Be joyful at your Feast" (Deuteronomy 16:14). The energy in the streets was palpable, and Shlomo gripped his father's hand with excitement.

"Everyone seems so happy, Aba!"

Lulav

His father grinned and ruffled Shlomo's hair. "And why not, Son? God has cleansed our sins and blessed our harvest. Now he invites us to his temple with offerings in our hands and praise on our lips! When I was a boy, this was my favorite week of the year, Shlomo. My brothers and I would help put up a booth for our family to live in, and at night your grandfather would fill our ears with stories of the Israelites' march through the desert."

A small sound from the back of Ima's throat caused their Aba to clamp his lips into a sheepish smile. He craned his neck purposefully left and right and said, "But the stories can wait. Now you and Miriam keep your eyes open for a patch of ground where we can set up our own booth."

A few hours later, they sat under the boughs of their own shelter, gathered around a pot of couscous and samples of the summer harvest—olives swimming in finely pressed oil, plump raisins, and the children's favorite: a drizzle of date syrup, thick, dark, and sweet. A blast of trumpets sounded from the temple mount, announcing the start of the weeklong festival. Aba filled the evening with well-embroidered accounts of Moses and Aaron and the Israelites' escape from Egypt. "For 40 years God's people lived in tents a little like these and wandered the desert. Yet God never forgot them; even their sandals did not wear out (Deuteronomy 29:5). And we, like they, are just pilgrims on this earth; each day closer to our heavenly home."

Finally Ima hushed them. Miriam and Shlomo lay back on their mats, gazing through the gaps of their roof at a full moon that drowned the stars and striped their faces with bars of light.

The night passed quickly. Before first light, Ima shook the children awake. She tied small woven bags to their waists and filled them with figs and olives, saying, "No one should appear before the LORD empty-handed!" They joined the hundreds of pilgrims already climbing the steep road to the temple mount, each one carrying their harvest offering and a tall, thin bouquet, or *lulav*, of willow, myrtle, and palm. A strong voice cut through the clamor of the crowd, singing the words of a familiar psalm. Aba quickly joined in, and soon the air vibrated with voices:

> *"The God of glory thunders,*
> *And in his temple all cry, 'Glory!'*
> *The LORD is enthroned as King forever.*
> *The LORD gives strength to his people;*
> *The LORD blesses his people with peace."*
> (Psalm 29:3b,9b,10b,11)

Finally the slow procession reached the stairs leading up to the temple mount. Everywhere they looked there were priests dressed in white. Aba noticed Shlomo and Miriam's amazement and explained, "All 24 divisions of the priesthood are serving this week. There are many services and many, many sacrifices each day. All together, 70 bullocks, 14 rams, and 98 lambs will be sacrificed this week as commanded by God. And that is without counting the freewill sacrifices that are offered!"

A high stone wall loomed before them. White-robed men stood sentry at a massive pair of ornately carved doors. Aba leaned close to Shlomo's ear. "This is the East Gate, the main entrance to the temple. Those men are Levite gatekeepers. It is their duty to prevent anyone who is ceremonially unclean from entering."

Finally the gatekeepers ushered Shlomo's group through the East Gate and into the outer court. At the far end of the court, Shlomo could see the altar of burnt offering. Atop the altar, several priests were laying the morning sacrifice on the smouldering coals. A choir of Levites burst into song. Over the flutes, harps, cymbals, and trumpets, Shlomo could make out the words of a psalm.

> *With boughs in hand, join in the festal procession*
> *up to the horns of the altar.*

> Give thanks to the LORD, for he is good;
> his love endures forever.
>
> (Psalm 118:27b,29)

In response, the large crowd of worshipers shook their *lulavs* toward the altar—a rustling, green torrent of praise.

At the end of the week, Shlomo and his family joined the throngs of homeward bound pilgrims, their hearts replete with stories, songs, and sights that pointed to the providence of their awesome God.

Sacred silhouettes

Sometimes the Israelites added ceremonies not prescribed in the law. For example, in later temple times, water-pouring ceremonies took place each day of the Feast of Tabernacles. The Israelites asked God to provide his people with rain for the upcoming season. A priest drew water from the Pool of Siloam in a golden pitcher. As he carried it to the temple, the congregation who accompanied him recited Isaiah 12:3, "With joy you will draw water from the wells of salvation." It may have been at the close of one such ceremony that Jesus stood up and said, "If anyone is thirsty, let him come to me and drink. Whoever believes in me, as the Scripture has said, streams of living water will flow from within him" (John 7:37,38).

Another interesting historical note on this day of festive joy is found in Deuteronomy 31:9-13, which states that every seven years the law (whether the whole Torah or just parts of Deuteronomy is unclear) was to be publically read on the first day of the feast.

The Feast of Tabernacles points to the final harvest of souls on judgment day (Zechariah 14:5,16). Revelation 7:9,10 pictures a worldwide harvest of believers surrounding God's throne with palm branches in hand and loud praise on their lips. The hunger and thirst and scorching trials of their earthly pilgrimage have been swept away by God's hand, and he is prepared to "spread his tent over them" and "lead them to springs of living water" (Revelation 7:15,17). In heaven we won't just live in the same area code as God, we will live in his own tent. We'll be close enough for God to reach over and wipe the tears from our cheeks. No wonder the saints in heaven are singing!

Bible reading

Moses did everything just as the LORD commanded him.

So the tabernacle was set up on the first day of the first month in the second year. When Moses set up the tabernacle, he put the bases in place, erected the frames, inserted the crossbars and set up the posts. Then he spread the tent over the tabernacle and put the covering over the tent, as the LORD commanded him.

He took the Testimony and placed it in the ark, attached the poles to the ark and put the atonement cover over it. Then he brought the ark into the tabernacle and hung the shielding curtain and shielded the ark of the Testimony, as the LORD commanded him.

Moses placed the table in the Tent of Meeting on the north side of the tabernacle outside the curtain and set out the bread on it before the LORD, as the LORD commanded him.

He placed the lampstand in the Tent of Meeting opposite the table on the south side of the tabernacle and set up the lamps before the LORD, as the LORD commanded him.

Moses placed the gold altar in the Tent of Meeting in front of the curtain and burned fragrant incense on it, as the LORD commanded him. Then he put up the curtain at the entrance to the tabernacle.

He set the altar of burnt offering near the entrance to the tabernacle, the Tent of Meeting, and offered on it burnt offerings and grain offerings, as the LORD commanded him.

He placed the basin between the Tent of Meeting and the altar and put water in it for washing, and Moses and Aaron and his sons used it to wash their hands and feet. They washed whenever they entered the Tent of Meeting or approached the altar, as the LORD commanded Moses.

Then Moses set up the courtyard around the tabernacle and altar and put up the curtain at the entrance to the courtyard. And so Moses finished the work.

Then the cloud covered the Tent of Meeting, and the glory of the LORD filled the tabernacle. Moses could not enter the Tent of Meeting because the cloud had settled upon it, and the glory of the LORD filled the tabernacle.

In all the travels of the Israelites, whenever the cloud lifted from above the tabernacle, they would set out; but if the cloud did not lift, they did not set out—until the day it lifted. So the cloud of the LORD was over the tabernacle by day, and fire was in the cloud by night, in the sight of all the house of Israel during all their travels. (Exodus 40:16-38)

Exodus 25–27,30—Tabernacle and Furnishings
Exodus 36–38—Constructing the Tabernacle
Exodus 40—Setting Up the Tabernacle

The architecture of a place of worship can tell you a lot about what its congregation believes. For example, a mirror tops the altar in a Japanese Shinto shrine. Why? Because Shintoism teaches that gods dwell everywhere—in trees, rocks, and even in people. The mirror on the altar reminds the Shinto priest of the god within him.

God wanted the layout and articles in his tabernacle, and later in the temple, to impress certain spiritual truths on his people. Each of them in some way was to picture how God relates to us. Hebrews 8:5 tells us that this sanctuary was a "copy and shadow of what is in heaven." Accordingly, God gave Moses blueprints for the tabernacle with strict instructions not to deviate from them in the least.

The word *tabernacle* means "tent." God's first house on earth was a collapsible, moveable tent. But this was no Coleman easy-erect camping tent. Even its pegs were made of bronze (Exodus 38:30,31).

Solomon's temple replaced the tabernacle. The temple was a rectangular building of hewn stone surrounded by two courtyards, an inner one and an outer one. It was oriented east, facing the rising sun. Along the sides of the temple were three stories of meeting rooms, priests' apartments, and storage rooms for the sacred vessels. As a rule, Solomon's temple was double the size of the tabernacle. The furnishings were also all larger echoes of the ones in the tabernacle. The Holy Place in Solomon's temple was ornately furnished compared to the tabernacle, which had only the small altar of incense, a single lampstand, and the showbread table. (See more details on the temple in I Kings 6,7 and in 2 Chronicles 3,4.)

Here are some details about the articles in and around the tabernacle, in the basic order of presentation from Exodus.

Ark of the covenant. We introduced the ark in chapter 2 in connection with the Most Holy Place, where we focused on the atonement cover, which lay on top of the ark. There is more we can say. This gold-covered box was about the size of the coffee table in your

living room. If you were able to peek inside the ark during the time of the exodus, you would have seen a jar of manna, Aaron's staff, and the two stone tablets on which God had written his commandments. By Solomon's time, only the tablets remained in the ark; the other items were perhaps lost to the Philistines.

Ark of the Covenant

The table of presence. As the priests entered the Holy Place, they saw this table on their right. On the table were 12 large, flat loaves of bread, reminding the priests that they served on behalf of the 12 tribes of Israel. Every week fresh bread was made to replace the original loaves. The older loaves went to the priests as holy food. On this table were also dishes for incense and flagons and bowls for drink offerings (probably wine, Exodus 25:29).

The Table of Showbread

The golden lampstand. As the priests entered the Holy Place, they saw this hefty menorah on their left. Five feet high and fashioned from 132 pounds of gold,

Lampstand

the lampstand had seven lamps. Every evening a priest filled each lamp with fresh oil so it would burn throughout the night.

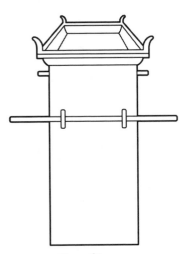

Altar of Incense

Bronze Basin

Altar of incense. This is the third and last article in the Holy Place, and it stood at the far end, in front of the curtain that hid the Most Holy Place. A priest offered incense on this golden altar twice a day. On the Day of Atonement, blood from the sin offerings was smeared on the horns of this altar.

Bronze basin. The bronze basin stood in the courtyard near the altar of burnt offering. The priests washed their hands and feet before they entered the sanctuary or made an offering. If they skipped this step, they would die. Exodus 38:8 says that the original bronze basin was made from the mirrors of the women who served at the entrance to the tabernacle. Solomon's sea of cast metal held 11,500 gallons of water—about the amount of a small, backyard, inground pool!

Gold. Silver. Bronze. Linen. Where did a couple million fleeing slaves come up with those kinds of materials to make the tabernacle and its furnishings? Remember, by the final plague, the desperate Egyptians couldn't get rid of God's people quickly enough. God moved the Egyptians to give the Israelites whatever they asked for, including jewels and clothing. Subsequently, all who were willing offered these treasures and their skills for the tabernacle project. In fact, they brought so much that they had to be restrained from bringing more (Exodus 36:6,7)!

Overseeing the work were two master craftsmen and teachers, Oho-liab and Bezalel. Under them was a skilled workforce. Moses gave credit where it was due: God chose the workers. God filled them with ability and skill.

What was the reason for a collapsible church? God's people were on the move; their sanctuary had to be portable. For 40 years, God led two million people—the number of inhabitants you would find in a large, present-day city—with a pillar of fire by night and a towering pillar of cloud by day. This pillar hung over the tabernacle. When God was ready to move on, he would lift his presence and the 12 tribes of Israel would break camp with military precision, according to their tribes and families. The tribe of Levi was in charge of assembling and disassembling the tabernacle. Twelve sturdy bulls carried the beams and curtains, though not the curtain that hung between the Holy Place and the Most Holy Place; this was used to cover the ark (Numbers 4:5). At the head of the procession, priests carried the ark of the covenant. The entire company followed the vanguard pillar of cloud.

After entering the Promised Land, the tabernacle was set up in Shiloh, where it stayed for four hundred years. Eli and his protégé, Samuel, ministered there. Later, King David moved the ark to a temporary tent in Jerusalem. He had the dream of building God a house, but he was a warrior with blood on his hands and God would not allow it (I Chronicles 28:3). However, just as God provided Moses with a blueprint of the tabernacle, he also inspired David to record every detail of the future temple with "plans . . . that the Spirit had put in his mind" (I Chronicles 28:12). God even chose the site: a threshing floor on a flat, breezy hilltop near the capital city of Jerusalem (I Chronicles 21:22; 22:1). This hill was also known as Mount Moriah (2 Chronicles 3:1): the very hill on which God had provided a ram for Abraham's sacrifice in place of his only son, Isaac (Genesis 22:13,14).

Finally, 480 years after the Israelites had fled from Egypt, David's son Solomon built a temple to house the ark. He conscripted a workforce of 153,000 men. They labored for seven years to erect this splendid building, quarrying stones from the pinkish-white limestone of Palestine and ferrying pine and cedar from Lebanon. The resulting temple was 4½ stories tall and beautiful to behold, yet it was not a testament to Solomon's ego but to God's grandeur and glory. Just as the Lord had once done at the dedication of the tabernacle, he demonstrated his divine acceptance of this building by sending a blaze of fire from heaven to consume the offerings sacrificed at the temple's dedication (2 Chronicles 7:1). It was Solomon's prayer that this temple would preserve the knowledge and worship of God in Israel and be a light to the Gentiles (1 Kings 8:41-43). But because of the sins of his people, God allowed his house to be destroyed by the Babylonians and again by the Romans.

God's original age requirement for a priest to serve at the tabernacle was 30 years old (Numbers 4:1-3). By David's time, Levites 20 years old and older were permitted to serve (1 Chronicles 23:24).

The story—Questions, questions

At noon, Shlomo and his family joined a dwindling group of pilgrims resting under the spreading branches of a tree. Overhead, a resilient autumn sun seared the edges of a towering white bank of clouds. A familiar voice hailed them, and they looked up to see Jeshua, a priest from their town of Hebron. Jeshua was 20 years old, now of age to begin his temple service. "You had a busy week, Jeshua! How was your first Feast of Tabernacles service?"

"I sang with the Levitical choir and helped carry many, many ashes away from the temple precinct. I have never seen so many sacrifices at once! And how is young Shlomo? Did you enjoy sleeping under the stars?"

Shlomo ducked his head, but curiosity won over shyness and he blurted, "Can you tell us what you saw at the temple? Did you go inside the Holy Place?"

Natan chuckled fondly as his son visibly swallowed further questions, but Jeshua regarded Shlomo with serious, dark eyes and said, "It is good when a child longs to know more about the things of God. Here, look at this."

The young priest knelt in the dust and took a sturdy twig between his fingers. He scratched a long rectangle into the dirt. "This is the temple courtyard, or outer court. You entered it from the East Gate. You saw the altar of burnt offering as you took part in the daily procession with your *lulavs.*"

"Yes! It was so tall I could see the top of it even over the heads of all those people!" said Shlomo, wonderingly.

"That altar is where we priests burnt your grain and animal offerings for the Lord this past week, as we do every day. On top of the altar is the perpetual fire, the fire God sent again when King Solomon dedicated the temple—just like the fire God sent to consume Aaron's offering on the day he was ordained as high priest. Coals are taken from the top of the altar to light the incense in the Holy Place. Ashes from the offerings are raked into a large pile in the middle of the altar; when the pile gets too big, it has to be carried away." Jeshua squeezed the muscles between his neck and shoulder and smiled ruefully. "That was my duty this week past."

Jeshua caught the flicker of disappointment that crossed Shlomo's face and said, "True, scraping ashes does not sound like a very important duty, but we seek to glorify God in all that we do, even in the humblest tasks."

Shlomo carefully avoided his father's gaze, fearing a homily about scouring out his Ima's cooking pots.

Jeshua's stick swirled in the dirt, and a smaller circle appeared near the altar. "This is the bronze laver, or wash basin. It's filled with water that we use to wash parts of the sacrifices and to cleanse our hands and feet before entering the sanctuary." He answered the question in Shlomo's eyes, "Cleansing our bodies before we worship reminds us to cleanse our hearts so we are ready to serve."

Jeshua traced a small rectangle inside the northernmost boundaries of the courtyard rectangle. "Here is the sacred sanctuary. Only priests are permitted to enter and only after proper preparation. It has two rooms. This room is the Holy Place." He divided the small rectangle in two. "And this section is the Most Holy Place. That's where God, who cannot be contained by the highest heavens, chooses to dwell on earth."

"Did you go inside the Holy Place?" asked Shlomo again.

"No, my duties didn't take me into the Holy Place during the feast. But my father described it to me many times when I was a boy like you, with a thirst for details."

Jeshua's eyes twinkled kindly at Shlomo. He scratched marks along both edges of the Holy Place. "These are the lampstands and tables of presence. In the first tabernacle there was only one of each. The single golden lampstand in the tabernacle was the only source of light in the sanctuary. You can imagine how dark and mysterious it must have been inside! The tabernacle lampstand was about as tall and heavy as your Aba. It had seven lamps—a sacred number that symbolizes God's covenant with us. Of course, King Solomon's temple is renowned for its majesty. It is twice the size of the original tabernacle. Now the walls of the Holy Place are lined with not one lampstand or table of presence, but with ten of each, five on each side of the sanctuary! Every evening, just as in the original tabernacle, a priest refills each of the lamps with fresh olive oil so that they burn through the night."

"And the tables of presence?" asked Shlomo. "How did your father describe them?"

"On each table in Solomon's temple there are 12 loaves of bread. Those 12 loaves remind us priests that we serve on behalf of the 12 tribes of Israel, our nation. We call them the bread of the face because we continuously keep the bread there, before God's face. Every Sabbath Day a priest replaces the old bread with new loaves. So God reminds us of his continual care for our needs."

"But that is not all that is hidden in the Holy Place," added Natan, never one to pass up a teachable moment. "In front of the door to the Most Holy Place is a small but very special altar, the altar of incense. Once a year on the Day of Atonement the high priest sprinkles the four horns of the altar with the blood of the sin offering. Pah! Pah! Pah! Pah!" Shlomo's father mimed the flicking of blood with his finger and thumb. "And incense is offered to the Lord there twice a day, during the morning and evening sacrifices. Jeshua, it is a great honor, is it not, to be the incensing priest?"

"That is so," agreed Jeshua. "It is a duty that is allotted to a priest only once in his lifetime. The smoke of the incense symbolizes the prayers of God's people ascending to heaven. I think you must know the psalm of David. . . ."

He broke off as Natan began to sing in a surprisingly sweet tenor voice: "May my prayer be set before you like incense; may the lifting up of my hands be like the evening sacrifice" (Psalm 141:2).

"You would not be out of place in a Levitical choir!" laughed Jeshua as he pressed the tip of his stick into the final, small square within the divided sanctuary.

"This, Shlomo, is the Most Holy Place. I only know from God's own description in the Torah what lies within, since none but the high priest can enter that room—and even he can only enter once a year on the Day of Atonement."

Jeshua's stick hovered over his diagram, and he flashed Shlomo a crooked smile. "Were I handier with a stick, you would see that the Most Holy Place is a perfect cube. This room represents heaven and God's perfection. It is also home to God's throne, the ark of the covenant." Jeshua scratched a small dent into the dirt. "On top of the ark is a cover that we call Yahweh's mercy seat. Two golden angels, cherubim, kneel atop either end of the mercy seat, bending toward each other so that their wingtips touch. It is from between these two cherubim that God spoke with Moses."

"And what is inside the ark of the covenant?" asked Shlomo.

"The two stone tablets of the Law. God made a covenant with us in the desert. He promised to bless us if we kept those laws. Of course, even our greatest efforts to obey God fail to meet his holy standards. The sacrifices show us that our sins deserve punishment. That is why we long for the Promised One to redeem us."

Shlomo's father waggled a finger in the air. "So you can see, Shlomo, why the cover of the ark is called the mercy seat. On the Day of Atonement, the high priest sprinkles blood on the cover of the ark, covering the laws that we have transgressed. It is a picture of how our sins are now hidden from God's eyes, blotted out."

With heavenly accuracy, a dollop of water splashed against the dusty diagram and soaked rapidly into the spot where the ark had been drawn. They looked up as more drops fell, and wide smiles spread among the group of pilgrims as the towering cloud overhead released the first of the autumn rains.

Sacred silhouettes

The tabernacle is a shadow that points first to God dwelling in human form. This happened when Christ became flesh and "tabernacled" among us (John 1:14).

In Hebrews 8:5 the tabernacle is also described as a "copy and shadow of what is in heaven." Does this mean, for example, that there is a literal incense altar in heaven? Probably not. We can assume the tabernacle paints an *impression* of heaven: the place where believers will be in God's presence. This is what Revelation 21:3 prophesies when it says, "The dwelling of God is with men, and he will live with them."

The architecture of our present-day churches bears some similarities to that of the tabernacle God designed. The altar reminds us of the ark of the covenant by symbolizing God's presence at our worship services. That is why the presiding minister usually faces the altar when he leads prayers. The candles on the altar remind us that Jesus is the Light of the world, just as the golden lampstand in the Holy Place may have foreshadowed.

The altar of burnt offering was a place of forgiveness and of refuge. Hanging front and center in most churches is another symbol of forgiveness and refuge: Jesus' cross.

Natan alluded to the ark of the covenant as a picture of the law (it housed the Ten Commandments) and gospel (sins against God's law were covered by the blood of the sacrifice). In the same way, the cross is a picture of law (God's judgment on all sin) and gospel (God's forgiveness won by Jesus' blood).

The bases on which the many posts in the tabernacle were set were cast from the silver that God had demanded from each adult Israelite as a ransom for his life. This atonement money was given in response to God's rescue from their enslavement in Egypt (Exodus 30:11-16; 38:25-28). How can we not think of the ransom Jesus paid to rescue us from sin's slavery? Our faith is built on the foundation of this ransom. We rest not on bases of perishable silver or gold but on that of the precious blood of Christ (1 Peter 1:18,19).

Finally, the bread and wine on the table of presence remind us of how through the bread and wine of Holy Communion, we have fellowship with God.

THE SABBATH

6

Bible reading

"Remember the Sabbath day by keeping it holy. Six days you shall labor and do all your work, but the seventh day is a Sabbath to the LORD your God. On it you shall not do any work, neither you, nor your son or daughter, nor your manservant or maidservant, nor your animals, nor the alien within your gates. For in six days the LORD made the heavens and the earth, the sea, and all that is in them, but he rested on the seventh day. Therefore the LORD blessed the Sabbath day and made it holy." (Exodus 20:8-11)

"Consecrate the fiftieth year and proclaim liberty throughout the land to all its inhabitants. It shall be a jubilee for you; each one of you is to return to his family property and each to his own clan. The fiftieth year shall be a jubilee for you; do not sow and do not reap what grows of itself or harvest the untended vines. For it is a jubilee and is to be holy for you; eat only what is taken directly from the fields.

"In this Year of Jubilee everyone is to return to his own property.

"If you sell land to one of your countrymen or buy any from him, do not take advantage of each other. You are to buy from your countryman on the basis of the number of years since the Jubilee. And he is to sell to you on the basis of the number of years left for harvesting crops. When the years are many, you are to increase the price, and when the years are few, you are to decrease the price, because what he is really selling you is the number of crops. Do not take advantage of each other, but fear your God. I am the LORD your God." (Leviticus 25:10-17)

Leviticus 25:1-7—The Sabbath Year

The system of keeping time in the Old Testament was based on cycles of the moon rather than on the solar calendar we use today. The Hebrew term for "month" is *chodesh*, which means "new moon." A month began when the first crescent of the waxing moon was

61

observed by the priests. They would signal the new month by blowing the ram's horn. The Israelites were not allowed to pass through the months as we 21st-century Christians often do, in a semiautomatic blur. For them, every new moon was a festival day observed by burnt offerings, sacrifices, and banquets (Numbers 29:6; I Samuel 20:5; I Chronicles 23:31). The New Moon Festival is often listed next to the Sabbath as an important religious observance that called to mind God's goodness (Numbers 10:10). Likewise, the middle of the month, or the full moon, was an important marker as well. Two important festivals took place under the full moon of midmonth: Passover and the Feast of Tabernacles.

It's interesting that the heavenly bodies dictate all intervals of time (seasons, days, and nights) except for our seven-day week. The seven-day week follows the lead of God at creation. In six days he fashioned planet Earth and the solar system in which it spins. On the seventh day, he rested from his work of creation (though not, of course, from his work of sustaining and preserving what he had made). In the Third Commandment, God told his people to *remember* the Sabbath Day, when God rested from creating. Deuteronomy 5:12-15 gives us God's second reason for the Sabbath. He wanted his people to *observe* the Sabbath as a reminder that he had brought them out of Egypt. We could boil down God's purpose for the Sabbath into these two points: (1) remember the Sabbath because I am your Creator, (2) observe the Sabbath because I am your Savior.

How was the Sabbath to be "remembered" and "observed"? For laypeople, the seventh day was primarily a day of rest. Outside of the sanctuary, no work was done at all. Practical application of the Sabbath rest is described in Exodus 16:11-30, when God gave the Israelites enough manna for two days so that they could rest on the Sabbath.

Days of rest were incorporated throughout the Jewish worship year in connection with annual festivals. On these days, work related to the people's secular occupations was forbidden. However, the Sabbath rest was a more complete rest than the rest on festival days. On the Sabbath Day *all* work was forbidden: there was to be no commerce, no menial household tasks such as kindling a fire, and no travel. God shows how serious he was about this ordinance in

Numbers 15:32-35, when a man was stoned to death for gathering wood on the Sabbath. By Jesus' day, the Pharisees forbade 39 distinct acts during the Sabbath!

Sabbath in the temple meant that two extra lambs were sacrificed along with the regular morning and evening sacrifices (Numbers 28:9,10) and a dozen fresh, warm loaves of bread were presented to God in the Holy Place.

God used the Sabbath as a weekly object lesson to teach his people that his relationship with them was not based on anything they could do. Rather it was based on what God had done and would do as their Creator and Savior. "Do nothing," God was announcing. "I made you and I will save you, in time (as in Egypt) and in eternity (through my Son)."

When we hear the term *Sabbath*, we usually think of the weekly day of rest. However, there were *three* kinds of Sabbaths that God wanted his people to observe: the regular Sabbath Day, the seven major festival days of rest, and the years of rest for the land called Sabbath Years. God calls all the Sabbaths "my Sabbaths" (Ezekiel 20:12, for example). He adds that these Sabbaths are a sign of the covenant between him and Israel. What comfort God intended his Sabbaths to bring to his people!

Just as God had rested on the seventh day and just as God's people had their weekly Sabbath rest, so too their farmland was to rest during the Sabbath Year: no sowing, reaping, pruning, or harvesting. God wasn't just recommending solid farming practices, he was teaching the Israelites that the land belonged to him and that the Israelites were to return it to him every seven years. In the Sabbath Year, debts were to be cancelled and slaves freed. God's people were to spend time studying his Word. God was particularly concerned that Israelite children would hear his Word and learn to fear and trust in him.

After seven Sabbath Years had passed for a total of 49 years, Israel was to observe a further celebration called the Jubilee Year. Some Bible scholars think that the Year of Jubilee ran concurrently with the 49th year. But it is also possible that the Year of Jubilee occurred in year 50, which meant that the land was to lie fallow for a second year—during both the Sabbath Year and the additional Year of Jubilee!

Resting on the Sabbath Day or letting the land rest in the Sabbath Year called for trust on the part of God's people. They could not be as ambitious or get as much work done as they may have wanted. The Jubilee Year took this to the next level. Just as God had freed his people from slavery and cancelled their debt of sin, so they were to free their fellow Israelites. During that year, creditors were to release debtors from their debts, return to them any land they had sold, and free any fellow Israelite who may have become another's servant during the previous 49 years. Such acts would have prevented serious poverty and class distinctions, which, in turn, would reinforce the fact that all Israelites were on the same level—redeemed sinners who looked to God alone for everything they needed.

Can you imagine following through on these directives—abandoning your office and your income, possibly even your property, not just for a two-week vacation but for a year or two? To quell the worries of those who wondered what they would eat during the fallow period, God promised such a bumper crop prior to the Sabbath Year that they could eat from it for three years (Leviticus 25:21)! This was no crooked salesman at the door, pocketing their money in exchange for a second-rate vacuum cleaner. This was their Creator, who longed to be tested in his promises so he could make good on them.

Sadly, there is no evidence in Scripture that either the Sabbath Year or the Year of Jubilee was ever practiced. Ezekiel 20 is a litany of God's laments over the Sabbaths that his people "profaned." And 2 Chronicles 36:21 suggests that the land finally rested only when God deported his people to Babylon: "The land enjoyed its sabbath rests; all the time of its desolation it rested, until the seventy years were completed in fulfillment of the word of the LORD spoken by Jeremiah."

The story—Sabbath celebration

"But it's pouring rain!" moaned Miriam, as Ima sent her out to forage for fresh coriander in the courtyard garden. The sky was grey. Encouraged by the moisture, vegetation had sprouted from every crevice in violent shades of green. Inside the house, Shlomo's mother was a whirlwind of pre-Sabbath activity, passing out rags and brooms, stationing her children next to the cooking coals to rotate the flatbread and stir the stew on her instruction. She was trailed by the pungent smell of roasted onions, coriander, and black cumin.

Shabbat, like all Jewish days, began at sunset, just as God had designed the first day: "And there was evening, and there was morning—the first day" (Genesis 1:5). From sunset on Friday to nightfall on Saturday, each devout Jewish family observed a full day of complete rest. Shlomo loved *Shabbat:* the sudden and complete relaxation from the weekly chores, the leisurely festive meals, the family discussions and study of the Torah. He couldn't understand why anyone would be tempted to break the Sabbath to gather wood, for example, like that unfortunate man in the Torah who had been stoned for his blasphemy against God's Sabbath rest. Not so enjoyable for Shlomo was the rag dipped in boiling water with which his Ima, having exhausted the supply of dust in the house, attacked his cheeks and ears and fingers, scrubbing until his skin throbbed.

"What's this, Shlomo, do you have a fever?" his father would tease, pinching his shining red cheeks.

Of course Shlomo knew from his conversations with Jeshua the priest that the Sabbath was not leisurely for everyone. Even as Shlomo and Miriam scurried about the house for their mother, the new division of priests and Levites was being assigned its duties on the temple mount. Fresh bread was being prepared for the table of presence. The altar would be cleansed after the evening sacrifice, and the keys and vessels would change hands between the old and new divisions. At sunset a trumpet signal would announce the official beginning of the Sabbath. A group of priests would carry warm piles of fresh bread and dishes of incense into the Holy Place. And as Shlomo and his family sat down to their evening meal, the priests in the temple would be sharing the older loaves of bread that had been removed from the table of presence.

Jeshua had also described how the morning sacrifice on the Sabbath Day started later than usual so more worshipers could attend, wearing their festive garments and carrying offerings. The morning sacrifice, along with the additional Sabbath offering of two lambs, was performed by the previous division of priests. They would not leave for home until the Sabbath was over, but the new division of priests would perform the evening sacrifice.

As sunset approached, Ima gathered the lamps in the house, cupping her hand around each to shield the small flames that quivered to life. She called the children, and they sat at Aba's feet, their eyes fixed on the tiny, trembling tongues of fire in the lamps. Aba began to recite from the Torah.

"*Remember* the Sabbath day by keeping it holy. Six days you shall labor and do all your work, but the seventh day is a Sabbath to the LORD your God. On it you shall not do any work. . . . For in six days the LORD made the heavens and the earth, the sea, and all that is in them, but he rested on the seventh day. Therefore the LORD blessed the Sabbath day and made it holy" (Exodus 20:8-11).

Aba paused, letting the silence swell before continuing. "So God gave his command to Moses at Sinai, linking our Sabbath rest with his own rest at creation. But 40 years later, when Moses repeated this command in his farewell address to the Israelites, he linked *Shabbat* to the rescue of our forefathers from Egypt. 'Remember that you were slaves in Egypt and that the LORD your God brought you out of there with a mighty hand and an outstretched arm. Therefore the LORD your God has commanded you to *observe* the Sabbath day' (Deuteronomy 5:15).

"And so each week at *Shabbat* we are reminded that God is both our Creator who gives us rest and our Savior who rescues us."

Their father raised his hands and pronounced a blessing on the food gently steaming on the low table. Soon the little room was filled with the sounds of a family sharing food and enjoying one another's company late into the night.

Sacred silhouettes

God was serious about his Old Testament Sabbaths because they were a sign of his covenant. God's Sabbaths foreshadowed the rest from guilt and grief over sin that Jesus would bring (Matthew 11:28,29; Hebrews 4:9,10). Isaiah 61:1-3 prophesied a *spiritual* Year of Jubilee, a "year of the LORD's favor," in which God himself would free his people from their debt to him and release them from sin's slavery. Jesus himself told us when Isaiah's prophecy was fulfilled. When he was observing the Sabbath in his hometown synagogue and it was his turn to read, he unrolled the Isaiah 61 scroll and read Isaiah 61:1-3. With all eyes fastened on him, he announced: "Today this scripture is fulfilled in your hearing" (Luke 4:21).

Jesus fulfilled the Sabbath law by giving rest to the whole world. And when this present age is over, believers will enjoy a final, eternal Sabbath. Then we will not necessarily toss aside the tools of our trade but the tools of the tempter: pain and sorrow and death. How we long for that Sabbath!

We might shake our heads at the wayward Israelites who consistently profaned God's Sabbaths with idolatry and faithlessness. But if we examine our hearts honestly, we will see that we often have done the same. Our Sunday worship is not the New Testament version of the Sabbath, but it shares a similar purpose. It calls to mind our Creator and Savior and his work on our behalf. There we are invited to rest in him and to receive the *New* Covenant in Holy Communion. What joy to hear God's command to put down our spiritual struggles and simply enjoy his forgiveness.

7   **THE PRIESTHOOD**

Bible reading

The LORD said to Moses, "Bring Aaron and his sons, their garments, the anointing oil, the bull for the sin offering, the two rams and the basket containing bread made without yeast, and gather the entire assembly at the entrance to the Tent of Meeting." Moses did as the LORD commanded him, and the assembly gathered at the entrance to the Tent of Meeting.

Moses said to the assembly, "This is what the LORD has commanded to be done." Then Moses brought Aaron and his sons forward and washed them with water. He put the tunic on Aaron, tied the sash around him, clothed him with the robe and put the ephod on him. He also tied the ephod to him by its skillfully woven waistband; so it was fastened on him. He placed the breastpiece on him and put the Urim and Thummim in the breastpiece. Then he placed the turban on Aaron's head and set the gold plate, the sacred diadem, on the front of it, as the LORD commanded Moses. (Leviticus 8:1-9)

Leviticus 8–10—Ordination of Aaron and His Sons
Numbers 8:5-19—Dedication of Levites
Numbers 4:4-49—Duties of the Levite Clans
Leviticus 7:28-38—The Priests' Share of the Offerings
Leviticus 21—Rules to Set Apart Priests

If you don't know the law or how a courtroom functions, you probably shouldn't represent yourself in court. Arranging for a competent lawyer to represent you may prevent you from digging yourself deeper into trouble. In Exodus 20:18,19, God's voice echoed from the peak of Sinai like the strike of a judge's gavel as he spoke the Ten Commandments. The Israelites could not bear this direct communication. They begged for a representative, a mediator between them and God, lest they die. Moses temporarily filled the bill, but later God gave the privileged role of mediator to the Levite priests, of whom Aaron and his sons were the first. Were there such a document as a Levitical job description, it might look like this:

* * * *

Job Title: Full-time Public Servants

Employer: God

Beneficiaries: The 12 tribes of Israel

Qualified Personnel: Levites ages 30-50 (older men may apply if there is a need), following a 5-year apprenticeship (Numbers 4:47,48; 8:23-26). Levites ages 20 and older will be permitted to serve once the ark of the covenant has a permanent home (1 Chronicles 23:24-27). *Special note: Members of the other 11 tribes of Israel need not apply.*

Basis for Qualification: All Levites were set apart for duty when they rallied to Moses and Aaron after the golden calf incident (Exodus 32:1-29). In recognition of their loyalty, God consecrated the Levites to serve in the tabernacle. They now replace the firstborn sons of all the tribes, whom God had originally claimed for service when he spared them in Egypt (Numbers 3:11-13). *Special note: All parents now pay a redemption price of five shekels for their firstborn sons since the Levites have been taken in exchange. This redemption money belongs to Aaron and his sons (Exodus 34:20; Numbers 3:46-48).*

Job Description: Levites are divided into priests and nonpriests, each with distinct duties.

Nonpriestly duties: Assist the priests, watch the entrance to the tabernacle and guard it, teach and judge, take part in the choir and orchestra, bake bread for Holy Place, transport tabernacle furniture during exodus. *Special note: Tabernacle transportation duties are divided between the three clans of Levi, descended from Levi's sons. Only apply for a job permitted to your clan (1 Chronicles 23:6). Gershonites carry the curtains; Kohathites carry the holy vessels (but only after priests have covered them or you will die! [Numbers 4:20; 18:3]); Merarites carry the posts.*

Priestly duties: Represent the people before God with sacrifices and prayers, and represent God before the people by pronouncing his blessings. *Special note: Only apply if you are a direct descendant of Aaron of the clan of Kohath. As a general rule, only firstborn sons can become high priests. This is a* lifelong *position.*

Part-time Temple Duty: Moses' census indicated there were 8,580 Levites of service age during the exodus (Numbers 4:47,48). Today there are about 38,000 Levites. Under King David the priesthood was organized into 24 divisions. Each division serves a week at a time, from Sabbath to Sabbath. Smaller family groups within each division will take turns conducting the daily temple service of that particular week.

Pay and Benefits: You may be paid with any of the following tenders:

Land: You will not receive an inheritance, for the LORD is your inheritance. However, to enable you to serve on a full-time basis, God has set aside 48 Levitical cities where you will live when not serving in the sanctuary.

Food: The bulk of the grain offerings and portions of certain sacrifices will be shared among the Levites (Leviticus 7:28-36). Enjoy this food in a proper manner, as it is holy food committed to the Lord.

Money: Redemption money belongs to the priests. Ten percent of Israel's income (a tithe) belongs to the Levites. The Levites are to turn over ten percent of this portion to the priesthood. In addition, every third year a tithe will be collected in the towns and distributed to local Levites and the poor (Deuteronomy 14:22-29; 26:1-15).

Additional Requirements for Priestly Levites

Because you are full-time public ministers and representatives of a holy God, you will be held to high standards of living. Please note the following details:

Family: You may marry and have children. However, you must maintain your holy status by not marrying divorcees or former prostitutes. A high priest is further restricted from marrying a widow, since she is no longer a virgin (Leviticus 21:13-15). Your family will also be held to a high standard of moral living. Any children who bring disgrace to the priesthood will be punished by death (Leviticus 21:9).

Handling a death in the family: Be advised that priests may have no contact with dead bodies, except to prepare and bury the bodies of blood relatives (parents, children, siblings, unmarried sisters, according to Leviticus 21:1-3). But a high priest may not defile himself for anyone. Nor may a high priest take part in a public display of grief (Leviticus 21:10,11).

Bodily deformities: If you have a bodily blemish or deformity, you will not be allowed to serve in any capacity at the altar of burnt offering or in the Holy Place. You will not be allowed to offer sacrifices or incense. However, you may perform other tasks in the sanctuary and you are permitted to eat food from various offerings.

Miscellaneous: You are not to drink alcohol while on duty. You are not to shave your head, trim your beard, or cut yourself, for these actions are associated with pagan mourning rituals (Leviticus 10:9; 21:5).

No task undertaken within your capacity as Levites is to be considered menial.

Everything you do will be to the glory of God!

✳ ✳ ✳ ✳

In Leviticus 10:11 God charters Aaron to teach the Israelites all the decrees that he had spoken through Moses. In fact, the book of Leviticus was really a public textbook for all God's people to study and live by. The Bible doesn't tell us much about the form of instruction that occurred in the towns. Ideally, Levitical cities were centers of Bible learning and proper worship practices for each tribe. The vignettes in this book present this instruction as if it occurred both formally and informally, led by "off-duty" priests and Levites. In practice, however, it seems that biblical instruction often was either lacking or ignored, since even the major holidays and sabbatical years were seldom observed properly (Ezekiel 22:26-29).

The story—Shlomo quizzes Jeshua

The week had gone quickly. Another *Shabbat* would soon begin. Jeshua was at home, anticipating his first week of service at the temple. There he would join the rest of his division to carry out their sacred responsibilities in God's house. He sat in the doorway of his house, watching the steady rain create muddy channels in the alleyway outside. A small, hunchbacked figure moved, crablike, through the rain, swerving between puddles. As the figure came closer, Jeshua recognized young Shlomo. The boy hugged a small woven bag to his chest, his body awkwardly bent to shield it from the rain. As he neared Jeshua's house, the boy called out, "Shalom! My mother has sent some bread for you to take on your trip into Jerusalem tomorrow."

"Shalom, Shlomo!" Jeshua took the proffered bag, which was mostly dry and emitted the warm smell of fresh flatbread. "You are wet through. Come in and dry off."

Jeshua watched with amusement as Shlomo stood, storklike, and ran his bare foot along his opposite leg, pushing down thin rivulets of mud. He switched feet and repeated the process, and then he scrubbed his head dry with the rag Jeshua held out to him.

"So what is my eager student studying these days?" asked Jeshua, reclining at a small table and patting the cushion next to him.

"Aba is teaching me of the time of the exodus and how the Lord chose Aaron to be high priest for the people of Israel. Aba says this shows the greatness of God's mercy, since Aaron had led the people away from God by making an idol."

"Your Aba is right. How great is our sin; how much greater is the Lord's mercy!"

"Jeshua, why did God give Israel a high priest in the desert? They had never had a tabernacle or priests before; not in Egypt or before that either."

"That is true, Shlomo. However, our forefathers did offer sacrifices to God. Consider Abel's firstfruits offering, Noah's thank offering after the flood, and Abraham's burnt offering of a ram on Mount Moriah. God in his wisdom decided that the exodus was the right time to establish a specific place and system of worship. For 40 days, Moses sat on the mountaintop with God, receiving God's instructions. As you know, when Moses finally climbed down Sinai, he found Aaron and the Israelites spreading out their hands to a foreign god! But the tribe of Levi, to which Aaron and Moses belonged, rallied to the Lord, strapping on their swords and felling the impenitent idolaters. Three thousand lost their lives that day—a great number, certainly, but still only a fraction of those who had offended God."

Jeshua shook his head slowly and continued. "No, their punishment was not as severe as it might have been. And because the Levites placed God above men, even kinsmen, God set them apart to serve him in his sanctuary. And in his great mercy, he gave the office of priesthood to Aaron and his descendants. Aaron became high priest while he still burned with shame over his sin! We priests do well to remember that our office is a gift that we have not earned and that we execute in deepest humility."

At this, Jeshua fell silent for so long, his brow painfully creased, that Shlomo made a slight motion to leave. Jeshua looked up with a rueful smile.

"I'm sorry, Shlomo. I cannot think of the priesthood without wondering what our future is. What upheaval we have already seen since Solomon's death and the split of the kingdom! Here in Judah, King Rehoboam has so far adhered to the ways of his father, Solomon. But consider what is happening north of Judah! In Israel, King Jeroboam has spat upon the ways of God. He has made refugees of many faithful priests and Levites. He has set up in their place his own priests, high places, and animal idols. I'm sure your father has pointed out the new faces here in Hebron, priests and Levites who have lost their inheritance in Israel. Our own King Rehoboam has welcomed them and their support. For now God is enthroned in Jerusalem. But his anger burns at the sin of his people, Shlomo. And no nation is mighty enough to withstand the anger of God."

It was a topic that Shlomo had heard his own parents discuss in half-whispers, and not one that he enjoyed. His mother had warned him not to overstay his welcome, but Shlomo was eager to lead the conversation in a happier direction.

"Can you tell me about Aaron's ordination as high priest?"

Jeshua slid a meditative forefinger down the bridge of his long nose, and his eyes pinched shut as he envisioned the scene.

"What a solemn occasion it must have been. The whole nation of Israel assembled before the tabernacle. Moses dressed Aaron and his sons in their priestly garb. He anointed the tabernacle and its furnishings with oil, and then he anointed Aaron's head with oil to consecrate him as high priest. Then Moses sacrificed a ram for Aaron's ordination. He splashed its blood against the altar and then painted it on Aaron and his sons: on their right ear, their right thumb, and on their right big toe. Perhaps this was to remind Aaron and his sons that they were to *hear* God's Word, *handle* well the holy things of God, and *walk* in God's way. Then Moses mixed the oil and blood and sprinkled it on their priestly clothes. The ordination service took seven days, and on the eighth day, Aaron assumed the office of high priest and was able to offer sacrifices."

Jeshua angled an eyebrow at Shlomo. "The sacrifice that always strikes me most is the sin offering God commanded Aaron to make, of a bull calf."

"Just like the golden calf that Aaron had made for the Israelites to worship!" said Shlomo, eyes wide.

"Yes. I wonder if Aaron felt the irony of it. Perhaps he did. Then, after sacrificing for himself, Aaron offered sacrifices for the people. As he spoke the words of blessing over the people, God's glory was suddenly visible: fire flamed from the column of cloud where God was present and burnt up the sacrifices on the altar, and the people fell facedown and shouted for joy. Forever afterward that very fire has burned on the altar, reminding us of Israel's constant state of grace."

"But Aba says things quickly went wrong. Aaron's sons dishonored the holy things of God and lost their lives!"

"Yes, and what a weight that must have put on Aaron's heart. He quickly learned how serious his role was as a priestly buffer between God and his people. He—like all the priests that have followed him—bore the sins of the people and offered sacrifices for them" (Exodus 28:38).

"What else do priests do?" asked Shlomo.

"You mean without weeds to pull and land to tend?" laughed Jeshua. "Well, when a particular priestly division is on duty, they travel to Jerusalem to stay at the temple and perform the temple services and sacrifices for the week. When they are not on duty, they live in their hometowns, Levitical cities that God assigned when the Israelites entered the Promised Land. Hebron here is one of them. And of course we priests keep busy when we are not at the temple by answering, as Eli did for Samuel, the long and tangled questions of curious young men like yourself."

Shlomo shot a worried glance at Jeshua's face and was relieved to see a teasing twinkle in the young priest's eyes. Jeshua continued.

"God also commissioned Aaron to teach the Israelites all the statutes God had spoken through Moses. That is why I spend much of my time teaching and being taught by my fellow Levites, and passing those instructions on to all of God's people, like you! The pagan practices encouraged by King Jeroboam in the north surround us too, as I'm sure your Ima and Aba have warned you. Pagan priests hide their rituals from the common people. But God's priests are to *share* their knowledge with God's people. In fact, that is the whole purpose of the Torah and why we each study it from infancy."

Shlomo nodded. He himself had spent lengthy hours under his father's tutelage. "But, Jeshua, if you don't own any land, how do you eat? I mean, if my Ima doesn't make you bread," he added.

"Well, since priests are keepers of God's house, God provides for us by assigning certain portions of the food and money offerings to us and our families. In this way we can devote ourselves fully to God's service, rather than earning a living by working the land. And speaking of God's service, I must really make some headway in my preparations to travel to Jerusalem for my first week of temple duty!"

Jeshua stood, smoothing his robes. "Thank you for reminding me of what an honor and gift the priesthood is. And thank your Ima for the bread. Gifts from families like yours are another wonderful way in which God provides for his priesthood."

Shlomo stepped into the courtyard and waved good-bye. The rain had stopped, and weakly steeped sunlight spilled through the heavy clouds. Jeshua's last view of the boy was of Shlomo steering a soggy path through all the puddles he had so carefully avoided on his way there.

Sacred silhouettes

The priests served as a sacred silhouette of Jesus, our perfect High Priest. Jesus is able to sympathize with our weaknesses. He was tempted in every way, just as we are, yet he was without sin (Hebrews 4:15). Like the priests, Jesus represents humanity before God; he taught, blessed, and prayed for us. He also offered a single sacrifice, himself, for the world. Because of Jesus, we can approach God's throne with confidence, knowing that we will not find judgment there but mercy and grace.

But it is difficult to reconcile this Old Testament office of dignity and respect with the priests we encounter in the New Testament. By Jesus' time, the priesthood could be purchased and was an office corrupted by bribes, greed, and power. Certainly these priests followed the Old Testament laws, but they were so mired in the rituals that they had lost their way. Consider how carefully the temple priests and Levites avoided becoming ceremonially unclean during Jesus' final Passover (John 18:28). They refused to enter the gentile Pilate's palace lest they be unfit for Sabbath observations. Yet, irony of ironies! bound and bruised between them in Pilate's courtyard was the promised Messiah, the very Son of God, whom they—not hired goons, but chief priests and Levites—had just spit on and beaten in the high priest's own living room (Mark 14:53-65)!

This perversion of the priesthood is not what the apostle Peter had in mind when he called Christians God's "royal priesthood" (I Peter 2:5,9). And that is what you are. In fact, you would be right to be overwhelmed with wonder at the honor and import of this title! Think of the Old Testament images it conveys: We are *cleansed* by Baptism, *anointed* with the Holy Spirit, and *sanctified* by Jesus' blood. We have *access to God* through his Son. We *offer* our bodies, gifts, and prayers as *sacrifices* that are acceptable to God through Jesus. We *intercede for others* with our prayers, and we *teach* others his deeds.

Not only that, God's royalty rubs off on us because we belong to the King! When I think of myself as a *royal* priest, all my actions and reactions change. Groan over my volunteer hours at God's house? How can I? Haphazardly prepare to receive Jesus' body and blood at Communion? Perish the thought! Dig for spare change when the offering plate is passed? Lip-synch the liturgy? Snooze through the sermon? Twitch through the prayers of intercession? No!

Think of it. We are priests, and kings too. These are roles we fill with trembling reverence!

THE FIVE SACRIFICES

Bible reading

*The LORD called to Moses and spoke to him from the Tent of Meeting.
He said, "Speak to the Israelites and say to them: 'When any of you
brings an offering to the LORD, bring as your offering an animal from
either the herd or the flock.*

*"'If the offering is a burnt offering from the herd, he is to offer a male
without defect. He must present it at the entrance to the Tent of Meeting
so that it will be acceptable to the LORD. He is to lay his hand on the
head of the burnt offering, and it will be accepted on his behalf to make
atonement for him. He is to slaughter the young bull before the LORD,
and then Aaron's sons the priests shall bring the blood and sprinkle it
against the altar on all sides at the entrance to the Tent of Meeting. He
is to skin the burnt offering and cut it into pieces. The sons of Aaron
the priest are to put fire on the altar and arrange wood on the fire.
Then Aaron's sons the priests shall arrange the pieces, including the head
and the fat, on the burning wood that is on the altar. He is to wash the
inner parts and the legs with water, and the priest is to burn all of it
on the altar. It is a burnt offering, an offering made by fire, an aroma
pleasing to the LORD.'" (Sacrifice 1, Leviticus 1:1-9)*

Leviticus 1–7—The Five Basic Sacrifices
Leviticus 22:17-33—Unacceptable Sacrifices
Numbers 15:22-25,30,31—Those Who Benefit From
the Sacrifices

A flight simulator reproduces conditions that pilots might face
on the job. This allows them to get hands-on experience without
exposing them to unnecessary risks. The sacrifices that God commanded his Old Testament people to perform worked in a similar
way. These sacrifices *simulated* a solution to the life-threatening condition of sin: a person sinned; the blood of an innocent animal was
shed; God's anger was deflected.

This simulated solution continued for 1,500 years until Jesus finally climbed into the cockpit, navigated through the turbulence of temptation, and—while carrying our cargo of sin—landed safely on the other side of death and judgment in order to present us with salvation.

Leviticus chapters 1–7 serve as a single unit containing God's instructions about offerings: *what* offerings to bring, *how* to bring them, *why* to bring them. A simple chart follows.

Bloody Sacrifices	Burnt Offerings and Fellowship Offerings	Express the covenant relationship
	Sin Offerings and Guilt Offerings	Restore the covenant relationship
Non-Bloody Sacrifices	Grain Offerings	Express thanksgiving

The burnt and fellowship offerings were used before Mt. Sinai. To these God added two more: the sin and guilt offerings. These two new sacrifices restored a broken relationship with a holy God. However, they came with a significant caveat: the sacrifices were for "oops" sins,[7] that is, sins committed unintentionally. Numbers chapter 15 makes it clear that God did not assign a specific sacrifice to cover the defiant, intentional sins of hardened sinners. Unrepentant sinners were to be *cut off* from the Israelite nation.

All five sacrifices involved items readily available to a nation of farmers and shepherds: meat from their domesticated animals, grain from their crops, olive oil from their groves, fruit syrup (honey) and wine from their orchards. These were mandatory sacrifices, but the

---

[7]John Lawrenz, class notes from Wisconsin Lutheran Seminary's 2003 summer quarter course on *Leviticus*.

Israelites could also bring voluntary burnt offerings, peace offerings, and grain offerings.

Whatever the Israelites brought to the Lord was to be their best, without defect or blemish. An animal sacrifice was a serious expense, considering the whole animal was to be offered and meat was a luxury that did not regularly find its way onto an Israelite's plate. How many of us would jump at the chance to turn a month's worth of premium groceries into smoke on an altar? Meeting God's demands required trust!

Although God always expected the best in an offering, he expected offerings only in proportion to the blessings he bestowed. He did not require the poor to bring the same offering as the rich, but he allowed them to substitute less costly material according to their means. This is how we know that Mary and Joseph were not prosperous: Jesus' mother presented a poor person's offering—two birds for her burnt and sin offerings—rather than a ram or lamb, which is what a more well-to-do person was to bring (Luke 2:22).

The grain offerings might seem a little out of place in the midst of all the blood offerings. Generally, they consisted of raw or cooked wheat flour or roasted grain, with the addition of olive oil, incense, and salt. Yeast and honey syrup were prohibited in the grain offering. This prohibition was partly practical, since yeast and fruit syrup were subject to fermentation and decay. However, their tendency to speed decay also means that yeast and syrup may have been omitted for a symbolic reason, to remind the Israelites that they were not to be corrupt or spread corruption. Salt, of course, was practical for the opposite reason, since it acted as a preservative. Symbolically, salt was eaten to establish a friendship in Bible times. Perhaps God wanted to demonstrate to his people that friendship with him had been solidified through their offering. The addition of incense reminded the worshiper that his prayers ascended to heaven with the smoke of the sacrifice (Psalm 141:2).

We who buy our bread presliced and packaged at the grocery store might think a grain offering is a subpar gift compared to an animal offering. But consider the family effort that went into preparing a grain offering according to God's command: planting, harvesting, threshing, and grinding the grain; sifting the flour; baking the bread; and producing the olive oil that had to be added. For the majority of Israelites, generating bread was their life's work! When they presented the fruit of this labor to God, they were acknowledging and thanking their heavenly provider.

Some offerings were also concluded by a drink offering of wine or oil, which the officiant poured either on the ground in front of the altar or on top of the burning sacrifice.

Portions of certain offerings were presented to God and then shared among the priests. Since this food came from God's altar, it was no longer ordinary bread or meat; it was "most holy" food (Leviticus 2:3) and was to be eaten in a holy place (the sanctuary) by those who were ceremonially clean. In this way God provided for the needs of the priests.

As an interesting sidenote, Jewish tradition claims ten miracles regularly occurred at the temple. One of these miracles was the complete absence of flies at the blood sacrifices. Another was that rain never extinguished the perpetual fire. (Though it breaks Jewish tradition, vignettes in this book do include flies. But rest assured that we never allow rain to prevail over the altar fire!)

The story—The sacrifices

Over the remains of dinner, Miriam and Shlomo plied their father with questions about Jeshua's duties in the week ahead. Chuckling, their father said, "It seems to me that we need to take a look at the Torah, which"—and here he held up a finger to forestall any protests—"is filled on the one hand with details of sin, guilt, blood, and fire, and on the other hand with details of fellowship, thanksgiving, and cleansing." He bent a wedge of pita with his right hand and used it to transport a dollop of creamy couscous to his mouth.

Miriam and Shlomo exchanged small, knowing smiles. A lecture was coming, but no dry and dusty explanation would suffice for their Aba. Despite their pretense at reluctance, they loved the stories their father wove from the Torah.

"Now," Natan continued with a dramatic throat clearing. "The Lord told Moses, 'Speak to the *Israelites* and say *to them*. . . .' These instructions about sacrifices are for YOU, Miriam and Shlomo, for *every* Israelite, so we know which offerings can be given to God and how and why they are to be given. And keep in mind, children," Natan continued with a lowered voice, leaning in close to them. "Unlike our pagan neighbors who feel the need to feed their gods, we do not bring our sacrifices to benefit Yahweh. He does not eat the flesh of bulls or drink the blood of goats (Psalm 50:13)! The sacrifices that God commands are for our benefit. Through these rituals of blood and fire God interacts with us. He allows us to bring our best from our fields and flocks, and when these are placed on his altar and their sweet smoke rises into the sky, our hearts, why, they are freed"—his hands flapped above his head like a misshapen bird—"of their heavy load of sin and guilt, for we know that God has accepted our offerings, according to his unfailing love."

"Aba," interrupted Miriam, with a seven-year-old's love of the literal. "Not every offering is bloody. What about the grain and drink offerings?"

Natan gave his little girl an indulgent wink. "Yes, Miriam, you are quite right. We ourselves spend the better part of the year growing and preparing grain for our food and its firstfruits for our God. We bring grain offerings to thank our provider. And of course grain and drink offerings are often included with sacrifices such as the burnt offering. When a family gives their grain offering, God's portion is burned. The rest is God's gift to the priests; it is their holy food. This week our neighbor Jeshua will be eating his share of the grain offering."

"But the blood sacrifices, Aba, tell us more of those!" said Shlomo eagerly.

"Ah, yes, my bloodthirsty young son! Of blood there is plenty to tell. God has made it plain to us that without the shedding of blood there is no forgiveness. And so we have four bloody sacrifices." He ticked them off on his stubby, calloused fingers. "The *Olah*, or burnt offering; the *Zevkah Shelameem*, or fellowship offering; the *Khattat*, or sin offering; and the *Asham*, or guilt offering. The first two, the burnt and fellowship offerings, were in use long before Mount Sinai and the giving of the Law. Those two offerings impress on us our bond with God."

"What do you mean, Aba?" the children wondered. Their father paused to pull off a section of raisin cake and passed the remainder to his children.

"Well, consider the burnt offering. A perfectly edible and delicious animal is laid on the burning logs of God's altar and consumed by fire. Only its smoke wafts upwards and is drawn into God's nostrils. Nothing is saved for stew; the animal is totally given over to God. Why does God want us to do this? Because it is the only appropriate response to God's total commitment to *us* and to his own promises."

"And the fellowship offering, Aba? How does that show our bond with God?" asked Shlomo.

"Because in the *Zevkah Shelameem* God invites his people to eat with him. We bring an animal offering. We give the best part of it, the fat, to God by turning it into a sweet aroma on his altar. A portion of the offering then goes to the priests as holy food. But the rest? The rest is spread before us like a banquet and is eaten in God's presence, as with a dear friend. Now, your Ima has played hostess to many a colorful friend of mine, but that is nothing compared to what our holy God does when he hosts us sinners!"

"What about the second pair of blood offerings, the sin and guilt offerings, Aba?"

"The *Khattat* and *Asham* were instituted by God at Mt. Sinai to *restore*, or *repair*, our bond with God. Despite our best intentions, we fall short of God's expectations. We may not mean to sin, but that is irrelevant. Sin is sin, and it must be paid for." Aiming a dramatic wink at their mother, Aba said, "I shudder to think what might befall your tender rumps were you to stroll around the house with mud squelching between your toes. Your mother is very handy with a broom, if you catch my meaning!"

The children giggled as their Ima shook the bristles of her broom at them with mock anger. Aba's playful tone turned solemn.

"Just as you would not dare to cross the threshold of your mother's house with dirty feet, so we cannot enter God's presence with sin sticking like mud to our hands and hearts. But because we are helpless to clean ourselves, God provides a way out of our sin with the *Khattat*, or sin offering. An animal's blood is spilled in our place. God graciously accepts this substitute. In this way the priest

83

makes atonement for the sin we have committed, and we are forgiven" (Leviticus 4:35).

Leaning back on his elbow, their Aba continued, "Finally, there is the *Asham*, the guilt offering. This sacrifice covers the guilt of our sin against one another, or against God's holy things or name. Perhaps we gave an inferior offering; perhaps we cheated or stole and lied under oath. These sins put us in debt to God. God demands a ram as compensation. And if anyone else is affected by our sin, we must pay them back in full and add to that a fifth of the total."

Their father shook his head solemnly and said, "Indeed, there is a man I know who stole two hundred shekels from his neighbor. He was frantic to pay back a debt he owed to his employer, who is known to be a harsh man."

Natan twiddled his beard as he allowed for a dramatic pause. Miriam broke the silence.

"What happened, Aba? Did he get caught?"

"He did, and it was a blessing. Otherwise, he might not have repented. Or he might have been eaten from the inside by a guilty conscience."

Even Ima had paused to listen. She said, "And he was already so desperate for money. What did he do about his debt?"

"Well, here is the best part of the tale. It shows how we simply cannot out-give God. The man returned the two hundred shekels he had stolen. He scraped together the extra 40 shekels required by the law. And then, what do you think? His fearsome employer heard of the sorry situation and forgave the man his debt! And he loaned his desperate employee the money he needed to purchase a ram for the *Asham*. All he ever said on the matter was that God had not given him so much in order for him to take the roof from over another man's head."

Ima pressed a broom and a rag into her children's hands. She gave her husband's cheek a brisk pat and announced, "Tomorrow night is *Shabbat*, another chance to soak up your Aba's wisdom! But now there is a floor to be swept and pots to scrub before bed and"— she silenced her children's groans with one arched eyebrow—"you need not fret: I will settle for a mere one hundred percent of your joyful service!"

✳ ✳ ✳ ✳

The next morning, under a glowering sky, a small parade of priests and Levites followed the road out of Hebron. They had planned their departure so that they would reach the Holy City of Jerusalem well before the trumpets blew to signal the commencement of *Shabbat,* the Sabbath. Shlomo and Miriam joined the pack of children who bounded, bare-limbed, through the puddles alongside the road and waved the men on their way. Jeshua acknowledged them through the drizzle with a crooked grin and lifted hand.

By early afternoon, Jeshua and his fellow Levites and priests had reached the city of Jerusalem. The sodden hems of their robes slapped their ankles. *Shabbat* would begin at sunset, and Jeshua's division of priests was to meet at the temple to share the duties of the Sabbath with the outgoing division of priests.

The temple trumpets had not yet sounded to signal the approaching Sabbath. At the threefold blast, all commerce and work would cease and Jerusalem's citizens would hurry home to begin their Sabbath preparation. With the lengthening afternoon, the vendors' voices had taken on a shrill edge; the customers hurried their bargains to a conclusion. Jeshua lingered in the marketplace, marveling at Jerusalem's vigor. In his mind, the city bubbled like boisterous yeast, so different from tranquil Hebron.

Jeshua paused by a stall that assaulted his ears and his nose with its medley of bleating, squawking, damp animals. As he watched, a shabbily wrapped woman exchanged a small handful of coins for two trussed pigeons and grasped them by their ankles so that they hung upside down, heads swiveling and feathers splayed in alarm. A man ran a careful hand across the quivering flank of a yellow-eyed goat, lifted its ears, and peered in its eyes. The man argued briefly with the vendor before handing over a purse of coins and dragging the protesting goat through a wet alleyway. Jeshua reflected on God's requirements for sin. Getting right with God was not cheap. And yet God dealt fairly with the poor; he demanded their best, but according to their means.

Jeshua wondered if he would meet the same woman or man later that week at the temple, to hear their heartfelt confession and to assist them in their sacrifice. As his week of service had approached, he had diligently reviewed the basic steps of offering a bloody sacrifice. First, the individual would present his sacrificial animal by bringing it to the sanctuary and laying his hand on its head. In this way the individual vouched that the animal belonged to him and was his substitute. Then, the individual would prepare the animal for sacrifice by personally slaughtering, skinning, dismembering, and washing it. What a powerful reminder to the individual that his transgression was serious: his sin had slain that innocent animal. And yet what a comforting reminder that God's love was also serious: God spared the individual's life by mercifully transferring the sinner's guilt to a substitute!

Jeshua continued his silent review. The priests on duty would carry out the final steps of the sacrifice. They would catch the blood of the animal and dash it against the altar, lay out its parts on the altar of burnt offering, and finally dispose of the unburned portions of the animal according to the type of sacrifice. Some sacrifices required parts to be carried outside the temple courts to be burned; other sacrifices allowed for certain parts of the animal to be given to the officiating priests as their due.

His reverie was interrupted when an older priest in his traveling group rested a gentle hand on Jeshua's shoulder. "Come, Jeshua, we do not want to linger too long. Our hands are needed on the temple mount."

Together they directed their steps toward the plateau on which the temple perched, overlooking the Kidron Valley. Not long after, the sonorous blare of trumpets rang out three times over the city, and with a final flurry, the tents of commerce were folded and the alleyways were emptied of people.

Sacred silhouettes

Picture believers who have been longing to expand the church they worship in. When they finally tack up an architect's blueprints, there is an electric excitement in the air! Even visitors to the church take notice of the blueprints. Those plans make an impression. They describe in detail what is to come. They draw attention to the goal.

But no one would look at those blueprints and consider the job done. You can't worship in a blueprint!

In the same way, God's Old Testament sacrifices were a blueprint that described in detail what Christ would come to do. Those rites inspired hope in the Israelites because of what they promised. They made a deep impression on the believers who participated in them. They even drew the attention of Israel's neighbors. But they were not the end product. They could not themselves forgive sins. Rather, they anticipated the forgiveness that the carpenter Messiah would build with the nails, wood, and suffering of the cross.

You learned in this chapter how each animal sacrifice was to be without blemish. So too the Lamb of God was without sin and therefore an acceptable sacrifice for the sins of the world. "You know that . . . you were redeemed . . . with the precious blood of Christ, a lamb without blemish or defect" (1 Peter 1:18,19).

And just as only those who sinned unintentionally or in weakness benefited from the Old Testament sacrifices, so Hebrews 10:26,27 warns us New Testament Christians, "If we deliberately keep on sinning after we have received the knowledge of the truth, *no sacrifice for sins is left*, but only a fearful expectation of judgment."

9 THE BURNT OFFERING

Bible reading

The LORD called to Moses and spoke to him from the Tent of Meeting. He said, "Speak to the Israelites and say to them: 'When any of you brings an offering to the LORD, bring as your offering an animal from either the herd or the flock.

"'If the offering is a burnt offering from the herd, he is to offer a male without defect. He must present it at the entrance to the Tent of Meeting so that it will be acceptable to the LORD. He is to lay his hand on the head of the burnt offering, and it will be accepted on his behalf to make atonement for him. He is to slaughter the young bull before the LORD, and then Aaron's sons the priests shall bring the blood and sprinkle it against the altar on all sides at the entrance to the Tent of Meeting. He is to skin the burnt offering and cut it into pieces. The sons of Aaron the priest are to put fire on the altar and arrange wood on the fire. Then Aaron's sons the priests shall arrange the pieces, including the head and the fat, on the burning wood that is on the altar. He is to wash the inner parts and the legs with water, and the priest is to burn all of it on the altar. It is a burnt offering, an offering made by fire, an aroma pleasing to the LORD.'" (Leviticus 1:1-9)

Leviticus 1—Procedure for the Burnt Offering

The first blood offering we will look at in detail is the burnt offering. The Hebrew term for this sacrifice is *Olah*, which means "the going up." "Going up" is exactly what happens in this sacrifice: the whole animal goes up in smoke, with an aroma that is pleasing to God. In a burnt offering, the worshiper could not quibble over which parts to burn and which to keep, like a customer at a meat counter who debates over which cut of beef to buy for the church potluck and which for the family table. By giving the whole animal over to be devoured by fire on God's altar, the worshiper was saying, "I am all yours, Lord. My body and all my abilities, my time and my possessions are from you and for you. I am completely devoted to you, my heavenly King." And as the penitent worshiper watched the fire consume his offering, he was also witnessing God's gracious presence and acceptance.

The daily burnt offering happened twice a day, in the morning and at twilight. The priests sacrificed this offering on behalf of the whole nation. The sacrifice was always an unblemished, year-old male lamb accompanied by a grain and drink offering. This daily offering remained on the smouldering altar throughout the night. In the morning a priest removed the greasy ashes of the burnt offering and carried them to a ceremonially clean place outside of the camp or sanctuary. New firewood was added to feed the altar flame.

A personal burnt offering expressed an individual's devotion or rededication to God. *Freewill* burnt offerings could be presented for the worshiper's personal benefit at any time. They could be offered by men or women but were probably usually offered by the head of the household for the benefit of his family. God *required* personal burnt offerings in certain circumstances, such as in the circumstance of a new mother or a cured leper whose quarantine was over. The type of animal sacrificed for the personal burnt offering depended on the worshiper's income bracket: it was always a male, and always unblemished, but it could be a bull, a sheep or goat, or a bird.

The worshiper was intimately involved in any personal blood sacrifice, including a burnt offering. He presented the animal to the priest, laying his hand on its head to indicate that it was his substitute. He then personally slaughtered, skinned, dismembered, and washed the dirty parts of the sacrificial animal (lower legs and intestines). There was no way a worshiper could avoid the lesson God was teaching: that forgiveness and bloodshed were intertwined. The blood, which suspended God's righteous anger, congealed between his toes, under his fingernails, and in the folds of his robes! At this point, the priests took over. They splashed the blood of the sacrifice against the sides of the altar. They placed the body parts on the altar fire, involving as many priests as necessary, depending on the size of the animal. The hide of a burnt offering was reserved for the priests, unless the offering had been made on their behalf.

The story—Jeshua's hard and joy-filled work

The Sabbath came to a close with the final throbbing notes of the temple musicians. Night spread across the sky like a bruise. Lingering worshipers turned homeward. A column of smoke rose from the altar of burnt offering in the inner courtyard and with it, the acrid smell of burnt meat from the evening sacrifice.

A group of men filed out of the temple precincts. This was the outgoing division of priests and Levites whose week's service was complete. The demands of a busy Sabbath in Solomon's temple were evident in the stiff gait of the older priests and Levites, but the young men had a spring in their step as they anticipated their reunion with their families.

Behind them, within the temple walls, a dozen Levites braced themselves against the massive temple gates and heaved them shut. Groups of Levites took up their night watches throughout the temple courts and at each gate. Stars shone out as the new division of priests gathered for the evening meal, sharing portions of the day's sacrifices and grain offerings before retiring for the night.

Jeshua stretched out on his mat on the floor. He stared into the darkness, not yet ready to sleep. He was thinking of his Aba, who would have been proud to see his son reach the age of service. A smile tugged at Jeshua's lips as he recalled his father's tolerant tutelage of him as a boy. Each day at dawn and dusk, Jeshua's father, a priest, had turned his small son to face distant Jerusalem. "It is time for the *Olah*, Jeshua, *'the going up,'*" his father would say, his worn hands resting on Jeshua's shoulders. "The priests in Jerusalem are rededicating you and all Israel to God with the burnt offering."

He and his father would stand together, eyes fixed on an imagined smudge of smoke in the northeast. Then Jeshua's father would explain how the priests selected two unblemished lambs each day to be wholly burned in the morning and evening sacrifice. Young Jeshua, accustomed to a simple breakfast of bread and olives and a dinner of spiced couscous, had been fascinated by the thought of offering Yahweh meat twice a day. "Why, Aba? What does God do with all that meat?"

His father had hidden a smile. "Our God never hungers or thirsts, Jeshua. We do not offer meat in order to feed our God, as our heathen neighbors do. God calls our sacrificial lambs 'offerings made by fire . . . an aroma pleasing to the LORD' " (Numbers 15:3).

Still concerned with his own clamoring stomach, young Jeshua had persisted, "Why does God want the lambs to be burned until only their *smell* is left? Why not share the *Olah* meat with the priests, as with other sacrifices?"

His father had patiently explained, "By offering the whole lamb, we are offering our whole lives to God. It is what Yahweh demanded of Abraham on Mount Moriah, the very plateau on which the temple now stands. Abraham was not to hold anything back, including his only son, Isaac! May we not hold anything back from our God either." His father had crouched so that he was eye-level with his son. "And don't forget, Jeshua, that Yahweh does not only demand, he also delivers. He brought us out of Egypt so that he might dwell among us and be our God. And one day he will send one greater than Moses to deliver us from our sins."

Fifteen years later, Jeshua was a young priest himself, like his father and forefathers: descendants of Aaron, of the clan of Kohath, son of Levi. And now Jeshua was in Jerusalem for his first temple service. Tomorrow he would take part in the *Olah* sacrifices, the solemn opening and closing of daily worship. He fell asleep with the words of the Sabbath psalm slipping through his mind: "It is good to praise the LORD . . . to proclaim your love in the morning and your faithfulness at night" (Psalm 92:1,2).

Jeshua's sleep was brief. The black sky's eastern cheek had barely blanched when the roomful of priests stirred. Men rose to wash and dress in preparation for the day's service. After Jeshua had bathed, he carefully drew on his priestly dress: white linen pants, a tunic, and a turban. As he secured the tunic around his waist with a colorful sash, the supervising priest arrived and led them into the court for the predawn inspection of the temple. The men circled the temple, their torch flames casting a lurching army of shadows on the stone walls beside them. Finding nothing amiss, they declared in a voice that echoed off the temple columns, "Shalom! All is peaceful!"

Morning slit a thin, bright seam along the horizon. Jeshua and his fellow priests formed a wide circle around a supervising priest, who would allot specific tasks to them for their day of temple service. The supervisor slowly counted them off until one group had been formed to clean the altar, another to prepare the sacrifice, and still another to tend to the lampstands and altar of incense in the Holy Place. Jeshua stood in the diminishing circle of priests. He watched intently as the lot was cast to burn incense on the golden altar in the Holy Place. A priest was allotted this duty only once in his life of service, and Jeshua could feel the anticipation of his fellow priests. Their eyes followed the supervisor's circuit until he stopped in front of an elderly priest.

"Nathanael. You will burn the incense," the supervisor said with a smile. Old Nathanael passed a trembling hand across his moist eyes, overwhelmed with the privilege that was his for the first, and last, time in his life.

The final lot was cast. Jeshua was chosen to assist those who would burn the sacrifice on the altar at the morning and evening service. But not yet. There was much to do before the sun rose and the morning sacrifice could be offered.

The first allotment of priests had already hurried off to the inner courtyard to cleanse the altar and prepare its fires before dawn. They paused beside the bronze basin, an enormous bowl of water borne on the backs of 12 bronze oxen. From this basin the priests applied water to their hands and feet so they would be ceremonially clean. Nearby, the altar of burnt offering loomed darkly, far above their heads. The priests ascended the altar by means of a wide ramp, their bare feet slapping softly on its cool surface. On top of the altar sat three woodpiles: one to burn offerings, a second to supply burning coals for the altar of incense, and a third pile that cast the only light in the courtyard, a flickering glow from which a dark rope of smoke unraveled. This was the perpetual fire of which Jeshua's father had often spoken.

"God himself commanded Moses to keep the fire on the altar continuously burning. Every morning the priest is to add firewood so that the fire will not go out. It always burns, son, even as the Israelite nation stands in the light of Yahweh's unending grace."

Armed with shovels and prongs, the priests scraped ashes from the fire, replenished the wood, and rearranged any meat from the

Sabbath sacrifices that had not fully burned, conscious that their seemingly menial duty was performed in service of a Holy God. As they finished their task, another priest descended from his lookout on a temple parapet and announced, "The sky is lit as far as Hebron!" At the mention of his hometown, Jeshua could almost feel his father's hands turning him to face Jerusalem as the sun climbed above the horizon and signaled the start of the morning sacrifice.

The click-clack of small hooves brought Jeshua back to the present. Two priests led a lamb across the courtyard toward the altar. They leaned over it with a torch, examining it for any defects that might have been overlooked. As they tied the sacrificial lamb beside the altar, the Levite gatekeepers slowly swung open the temple gates. Three trumpet blasts announced to the stirring city that the morning sacrifice was about to be offered. A small knot of worshipers had already filed in through the East Gate, a few with animals for personal offerings.

The sacrificing priest knelt and laid his hand on the lamb's head. He guided its head through a ring in the floor and then quickly drew his knife across its outstretched neck. A dark stream of blood splashed into a golden bowl held by his assistant. This priest dipped his finger into the bowl and flicked the warm blood along the sides of the altar. He tipped the rest of the blood against the base of the altar. The lamb was cut into parts and washed in one of the wheeled basins in the courtyard. The portions were then carried to the top of the altar and salted.

While the lamb was being sacrificed, another allotment of priests entered the Holy Place through folding doors overlaid with beaten gold and elaborately etched with cherubim and palm trees. They had been allotted the tasks of cleaning the altar of incense and preparing the lampstands. At the far end of the long, narrow room stood the altar of incense, its gold overlay burnished by the flickering light of ten lampstands that lined the sidewalls. One priest approached the altar and dipped a small shovel into its mound of soft grey ash. As he scooped out the ash, he released an aroma of frankincense into air already redolent with smoke and olive oil. A second priest tended to a golden lampstand that was as tall as he. Its flames had burned through the night, just as Yahweh of the covenant had not slumbered. The priest trimmed the wicks and refilled the seven flower-shaped lamps with fresh oil. He paused for a respectful moment, watching the flames quiver and then straighten, sending their thin plumes of smoke upwards. Shadows shrank before the flames' warm light. "Just as Yahweh's Spirit gives us light in the Torah," he thought, before worshipfully withdrawing along with the other priests.

Now it was old Nathanael's turn to slowly climb the steps to the Holy Place. The temple fell silent as those gathered in the court-yard awaited the moment that their prayers would rise like incense before God. Nathanael entered the Holy Place with a golden bowl that held smoldering coals from the altar of burnt offering. He spread the coals on the altar of incense; he then gathered a handful of fresh incense and allowed the grains to sift through his quivering fingers onto the small, golden altar. As the incense spilled across the burning coals, an aromatic cloud rose. Outside the Holy Place, Jeshua joined the priests and Levites and worshipers in prayer: "You are Jehovah; there is no God beside you. Let the burnt offerings of Israel and their prayer be accepted in love and let our service be pleasing to you. Bless us with your peace."[8]

And now came the heart of the morning service: the offering of the sacrifice on behalf of the Israelite nation. Jeshua's heart lurched under his linen tunic. He drew in a deep breath and offered a silent prayer. "Not just this lamb as an offering, Lord, but my mind and body too. 'A broken and contrite heart, O God, you will not despise'" (Psalm 51:17).

An elder ascended the altar, and Jeshua joined his fellow priests in handing him, one by one, the pieces of the sacrifice. The elder pressed his hands on each piece and then arranged them on the fire. The pieces spat and sizzled as they hit the coals, belching greasy clouds of smoke.

Above the crackle of roasting meat, Jeshua heard the fluting voice of old Nathanael. He was reciting the priestly blessing: "Jehovah

[8]Alfred Edersheim, *The Temple* (Grand Rapids: Eerdmans Publishing, 1972), pp. 168,169.

bless you and keep you. . . ." In a rumbling bass, Jeshua and the other Levites added their voices, ". . . Jehovah make his face shine on you and be gracious to you; Jehovah turn his face to you and give you peace" (see Numbers 6:24-26). The worshipers in the courtyard joyfully responded, "Blessed be the Lord God of Israel, from everlasting to everlasting!"

The elder who stood atop the altar added the grain offering to the fire, a handful of grain mixed with oil and incense. The drink offering followed: it was poured on top of the burning meat, where it vaporized in a hiss of rising steam. With a blast of trumpets and a clash of cymbals, a choir of Levites began to sing the daily temple psalm, a psalm that began and ended each new day.[9] Jeshua closed his eyes and listened to the familiar words.

> *"Great is the LORD and most worthy of praise.*
> *The LORD is faithful to all his promises*
> *and loving toward all he has made."*
> (Psalm 145:3a,13b)

"Yes," thought Jeshua. "Yes."

Sacred silhouettes

Like the lamb for the daily burnt offering, Jesus is a "lamb without blemish or defect" (1 Peter 1:19). Just as God was pleased with the aroma of a faithful sacrifice, so he was pleased with his Son who "gave himself up for us as a fragrant offering and sacrifice to God" (Ephesians 5:2).

Because of Jesus' perfect sacrifice, we Christians are "the aroma of Christ" through whom he "spreads everywhere the fragrance of the knowledge of him" (2 Corinthians 2:15,14). Just think—our every word and action as Christians is like the pleasing aroma of an Old Testament sacrifice, wafting along in our wake!

---

[9]According to the temple liturgy, Psalm 145 was used twice in the morning and once at night (John Brug, *A Commentary on Psalms 73–150* [Milwaukee: Northwestern Publishing House, 2005], p. 488).

While we New Testament Christians no longer need to offer animal sacrifices, Christ's love compels us to offer our bodies "as living sacrifices, holy and pleasing to God" as our "spiritual act of worship" (Romans 12:1).

The New Testament records the priest Zechariah's experience with offering incense at the altar in the Holy Place. In the midst of this rare privilege, the angel Gabriel appeared and announced that the priest's barren wife, Elizabeth, would have a son, John, who would prepare the way for the Lord (Luke 1:5-22).

THE FELLOWSHIP OFFERING

Bible reading

"If someone's offering is a fellowship offering, and he offers an animal from the herd, whether male or female, he is to present before the LORD an animal without defect." (Leviticus 3:1)

Leviticus 3:1-16—Procedure for the Fellowship Offering
Leviticus 7:11-21—Consumption of Fellowship Offerings
Leviticus 7:28-34—Priestly Allotment of Fellowship Offerings
Numbers 6:1-21—Fellowship Offerings to Conclude a Nazirite Vow

The fellowship offering is the second blood sacrifice we will examine. The Hebrew term for the fellowship offering is *Zevkah Shelameem*, which means "slaying for peace." This offering expressed the intimate connection, or fellowship, between God and his people. After the animal was slain and sin was dealt with, God invited his people to stay and eat with him! He was not a grim-faced host at this banquet, swatting the hand that reached for seconds, but a generous benefactor who delighted to share a festive meal with his people.

The fellowship offering was a voluntary, personal sacrifice. The only exception to this rule was on the Feast of Pentecost, when God *required* a public fellowship offering. Otherwise, no particular occasion was prescribed for this offering. The fellowship offering may have occurred most often at the three pilgrim festivals, providing a chief source of food—and a rare helping of animal protein—for the meals eaten on those special holy days.

Leviticus 7:12-18 describes three different purposes for offering this sacrifice:

1. As a **thank offering** given in gratitude for a specific blessing from God, such as deliverance from illness, trouble, or death (Psalm 116:17).

2. As a freewill offering given in general thanksgiving for God's blessings, such as a good crop (Deuteronomy 16:10).

3. As a votive offering, that is, an offering associated with a vow an Israelite made to the Lord. The Israelites promised to give God a gift in response to his deliverance or blessing. The bull slaughtered by Hannah and her husband, Elkanah, was likely a votive offering, given when Hannah fulfilled the vow she made when she begged God for a son (I Samuel 1:24-27).

As another example, the vow of the Nazirite was normally a temporary vow, at the conclusion of which an Israelite would bring a fellowship offering to the Lord. The specifics are described in Numbers 6:1-21. A Nazirite had to offer a ram as his fellowship sacrifice.

With the exception of a Nazirite, a worshiper could offer any unblemished animal, male or female, from herd or flock. The fellowship offering began in the same way as a burnt offering: the worshiper presented the animal at the sanctuary, placed his hand on its head, and slaughtered it. But there the ceremony took a new turn. The offerer with "his own hands" now piled the fatty parts of the animal onto its breast cage and "waved," or elevated, the breast and its contents before the Lord's altar (Leviticus 7:30). The priest then removed the fat from the brisket and burned it along with the kidney and liver of the animal. The breast and right thigh were given to the priests. The rest of the animal belonged to the worshiper. (Again there is a slight difference with a Nazirite fellowship offering: in that case, the breast, thigh, and shoulder were given to the priests.)

It may seem unusual to present God with fatty innards, something that most of us trim off and toss out. However, the fat was considered the choicest part of the animal. (Many in Asian cultures today would agree, since the fat soaks up juice and flavor when cooked.) Furthermore, many pagan religions claimed supernatural power from eating the fat of animals that had been sacrificed to a deity. God therefore demanded all the fat from all animals; Israelites were forbidden to eat it, or they would be cut off from their people (Leviticus 7:25).

God put a strict time limit on *when* the meal could be eaten: a thank offering was eaten the same day it was presented; the other two offerings could also be eaten on the following day. Any meat left by the third day had to be burned. Only those who were ceremonially clean could eat of the fellowship offering.

The story—Jeshua assists a Nazirite

The winter sun pulsed with surprising strength overhead. Jeshua wiped a sleeve across the sweat that prickled on his forehead. He and his priestly division were assisting in the daily sacrifices brought by Israelites who had come to unburden their sin and guilt. It was not clean work. His hands and linens were stained with blood, and his nostrils were clogged with the odor of sweating livestock and burning meat.

Jeshua heard a clamor in the outer courtyard, through which a man was leading an entourage of animals and people. An air of festivity surrounded them, but it was the man who caught Jeshua's attention. A riot of tangled hair spilled over the man's narrow shoulders. Jeshua recognized the marks of one who had taken the vow of a Nazirite and whose period of dedication was complete.

The Nazirite tugged two lambs along; behind him, one boy pulled and another pushed a reluctant ram and several women carried in baskets of grain and drink offerings and a small pyramid of loaves.

"Shalom!" The man raised his voice over the din of his companions. "Twelve months ago I took the vow of a Nazirite when my only daughter fell ill and almost died." His hand reached down automatically and found the curly head of a young girl, who tightened a chubby arm around his leg. "I cried out to God, and in my distress he answered me." He gave his daughter's round cheek a fond pinch, sending more color flooding to her face. "Now she blooms like a rose of Sharon! And, as I vowed, for the last year I have devoted myself to God, allowing him to fill my thoughts: no wine or grapes have crossed my lips, no razor has touched my head, and I have not been in the presence of a dead body. Today I bring with me a lamb for a sin offering, a lamb for a burnt offering, and a ram for a fellowship offering. God be praised; today my whole family and dearest friends are ceremonially clean and eager to share in the fellowship meal."

99

"*Baruch Hashem!* May God's name be praised!" echoed Jeshua, smiling broadly.

A second priest joined them to assist with the sacrifices; and after some shuffling of bodies, a space was cleared for the Nazirite and the two lambs for the sin and burnt offerings. The man placed his hands on each animal's head in turn, and then he knelt and tugged a knife across the lambs' necks in quick succession. Jeshua caught the blood in a vessel and carried it to the altar of burnt offering, dashing it against the perimeter of the altar so that it ran down the stones, adding its stain to the dark residue of past offerings.

The Nazirite bent to the slow task of dismembering the lambs and washing their parts. As Jeshua supervised the grisly chore, he reflected on God's directions for the fulfillment of a vow. *How well God knows our corrupt hearts,* he thought. This man had just dedicated an entire year to God, and yet God demanded a sin offering. There was no chance for this Nazirite to congratulate himself on the last 12 months when the first thing God required was a sacrifice for his sin!

Clouds heaped up on the horizon, but the sun, muscling westward, was still mercilessly hot. One by one, Jeshua carried raw slabs of meat up the altar ramp and slid them onto the coals. In the courtyard below, the Nazirite finally paused his exertions and stretched. With the sin offering and burnt offering complete, his sins had been atoned for and God had accepted him. The man turned to his little girl. She had long since vacated her post at his side and was now curled in her mother's lap, but her dark eyes never strayed from her Aba. Mindful of the blood and sweat that streaked his face, he directed a reassuring smile at his daughter.

"God in his mercy spared you, little one, and now I have fulfilled my vow to God. It is time for the *Zevkah Shelameem,* the slaying for peace. God will meet with us at this banquet without anger at our sins, as a loving host."

He bent over the ram, and his knife winked briefly in the sunlight before the ram went limp. Jeshua flicked this blood too against the altar, raising an iridescent army of swollen flies that circled lazily before reclaiming their stations. Jeshua watched as the Nazirite slowly dismembered the ram. The man's forearms were caked in blood, and his veins were knotted with effort. The Nazirite set aside the portions that God demanded—the fat, kidneys, and liver—heaping them into the breast cage of the ram. Arms trembling, the man lifted the breast cage with its mound of pearly fat and glistening organs, presenting them to God before his altar. An assisting priest collected the breast, the right thigh, and the shoulder of the ram; these would be shared among all the priests on duty. Only the fat and organs would be turned to smoke on the altar. Jeshua glanced at the little girl, who watched the procedures with wide brown eyes. A smile lit her face as her father swung her up in the air, declaring, "Now it is time for Aba to shave his hair!"

From the folds of her garment, the girl's mother handed her husband a newly honed razor, which he took and, without ceremony, sawed through his knotted locks. As they fell, his wife and daughter caught them in a cloth where they heaped up like a dark, limp animal.

When the Nazirite's head was clean-shaven, Jeshua collected the hair that had been dedicated to the Lord and the fatty portions of the ram. He climbed the large ramp to the top of the altar; the heat of the fire fanned his face and stung his eyes. He laid the hair directly on the coals, where it immediately smoldered and writhed before igniting in an acrid gust of smoke. On top of the hair, Jeshua placed God's fatty portions. An errant breeze delivered a pungent noseful of the combined offerings to the group that stood below the altar, and the little girl grimaced and clapped both hands over her face.

As Jeshua rejoined the group, he grinned at her. "In our noses it burns, but in God's nose it is a pleasing aroma." At her doubtful look, his smile grew even wider. A second priest hurried over with the boiled shoulder of the ram, which Jeshua placed in the Nazirite's hands, together with a cake and a wafer from his wife's basket. Together they elevated these things before the Lord. They belonged to God, and God in turn gave this holy food to his priests as their portion. The votive fellowship offering now complete, Jeshua addressed the family as they gathered their portion of meat and prepared to leave.

"Enjoy your fellowship meal this evening, knowing that your sin has been covered, God has accepted your offering, and he now invites you to be his guests at this holy meal."

The father hoisted his daughter to his shoulders and carried her out. Jeshua's last view was the little girl's chubby fingers running wonderingly over the top of her father's newly shorn head.

Sacred silhouettes

Jesus fulfilled all the functions of every sacrifice prescribed in the Old Testament. Our sin and guilt have been removed by the cross. God accepts us for Jesus' sake. And now Jesus invites us to a new and better fellowship meal: the banquet of his body and blood at Holy Communion. He is at once our feast and our host! And just as only those who were ritually clean were allowed to partake of the fellowship offering, so we will want to be properly prepared to receive the Lord's Supper (1 Corinthians 11:27-30).

The Hebrew term for a fellowship thank offering can be translated as a "sacrifice of praise." God never wanted his Old Testament people simply to go through the motions. He says in Psalm 50:23, "The one who offers *thanksgiving* as his sacrifice glorifies me."[10] The New Testament echoes this thought. "Through Jesus, therefore, let us continually offer to God *a sacrifice of praise*—the fruit of lips that confess his name" (Hebrews 13:15). God is pleased to receive sacrifices from his saints: not bowls brimming with blood but lives overflowing with praise.

[10]Translation by Dr. John Brug, *A Commentary on Psalms 1-72*, p. 500.

THE SIN OFFERING

Bible reading

The LORD said to Moses, "Say to the Israelites: 'When anyone sins unintentionally and does what is forbidden in any of the LORD's commands—

"'If the anointed priest sins, bringing guilt on the people, he must bring to the LORD a young bull without defect as a sin offering for the sin he has committed.'" (Leviticus 4:1-3)

Leviticus 4:1-35—Procedure for Sin Offering
Leviticus 5:1-13—Sins That Require a Confession and Sin Offering
Leviticus 6:24-30—Proper Handling of a Sin Offering
Leviticus 12:1-8—Purification After Childbirth
Leviticus 1:14-17—Offering of Birds

The sin offering is the third blood sacrifice we will examine. This offering acknowledged that a particular sin threatened the relationship between the sinner and God. The Hebrew term for the sin offering is *Khattat,* which means "to purge." The purpose of this offering was to cleanse worshipers from unintentional sin, that is, sin not committed in hardened unbelief (Numbers 15:30). This forgiveness allowed worshipers to reenter God's presence and restored their covenant relationship with God.

Our society regards "oops" sins with a more lenient eye than willful sins. God, on the other hand, regards all sins as a falling short of his requirement of perfect obedience. Whether or not we *meant* to sin is irrelevant. Sin is sin and must be paid for.

Leviticus chapter 5 opens with three scenarios of unintentional sins:

1. Failure to testify in court, if one is a witness
2. Failure to purify oneself after contact with an unclean animal or person

3. Failure to keep a carelessly made oath (Psalm 15:1a,4b, "LORD, who may dwell in your sanctuary? [He] who keeps his oath even when it hurts")

Entering God's presence in these cases without a sin offering would contaminate the sanctuary and call down God's wrath.

Though God doesn't grade sin, he did have different requirements for atoning for various sins. The requirements changed depending on *who* had sinned. If the high priest sinned or if the entire community sinned, God required a bull as a sacrifice. In both cases, blood from the sin offering was sprinkled on the curtain in front of the Most Holy Place. The remaining blood was painted on the four horns of the altar of burnt offering and poured out at its base. The sin did not only stain the person but also God's sanctuary. (If this procedure sounds familiar, it should. The Day of Atonement offerings were really versions of the sin offering expanded to cover the sins of the high priest and the whole Israelite community.)

If a leader sinned, God required a male goat as a sacrifice. In this case, the blood from the sin offering did not enter the Holy Place but was painted on the horns of the altar of burnt offering and poured at its base.

If a layperson sinned, God required a female goat or sheep as a sacrifice. But a poor layperson could bring two doves or pigeons. If even these were beyond his means, he could substitute a portion of fine flour as his sin offering. Regardless of who sinned, a specific confession was made prior to offering the sacrifice (Leviticus 5:5).

The sin offering was available to any Israelite who realized his error and was in need of forgiveness. Although it was intended for unintentional sins, that does not mean planned and defiant sins could not be forgiven. Consider King David's romance with sin. In weakness, he plotted out a path of adultery and murder that eventually sucked him dry, both spiritually and physically. He repented and received God's forgiveness. Who of us couldn't echo with David the words of Psalm 130:3,4a, "If you, O LORD, kept a record of sins, O Lord, who could stand? But with you there is forgiveness"?

You may be curious about why certain offerings are called most holy, such as the meat and the blood of the sin offering (Leviticus 6:24-30). Their holiness was the result of what they were being used for. That is, when a common animal was offered on God's altar, it was transformed into a holy substance. Furthermore, this holiness stuck to whoever or whatever touched the sacrifice.

In Leviticus chapter 6, God gave directions to avoid desecrating this holy meat or blood. The meat or blood was to be found only where God intended. If the priests' clothes were spattered with the holy blood, they were to be laundered in the sanctuary. If the holy meat was cooked in a porous clay pot, the pot had to be destroyed since it might have absorbed some of its contents. If a copper pot was used, it had to be scoured clean of any clingy remnants of the holy meat.

A priest could not benefit from his own sin offerings by eating them; the meat was incinerated "outside the camp" (in other words, outside of the ritually clean place surrounding the tabernacle). However, the officiating priest could eat the meat of a private sin offering in the sanctuary courtyard, a "holy place."

Another situation that required a sin offering was the purification rites of a new mother. After giving birth, a woman's postnatal discharge made her unclean, just as menstrual blood did. She was to stay in seclusion for a set amount of time that depended on the gender of her baby. If she delivered a baby boy, she had to spend 7 days in social seclusion; if she had a daughter, she was to spend 14 days in seclusion. During this time she could not have intercourse, make meals, or do any other housework.

The same ritual washing that closed a menstrual cycle concluded this period of seclusion. Then the new mother was able to resume her normal domestic role. If she had given birth to a son, his circumcision followed this period when he was eight days old.

However, the mother was still unclean and barred from the sanctuary until her complete "term" had been served, totaling 40 days after birthing a son and 80 days after birthing a daughter. When her quarantine was complete, she was to go to the sanctuary to offer sacrifices for purification.

The story—Jeshua continues his work at the temple

Jeshua glanced at the sloping sun. It had burned off its ferocity and now wore a mantle of dark rain clouds. Soon preparations would begin for the evening sacrifice.

For a moment, Jeshua's shoulders sagged with a fatigue that was something more than mere physical exhaustion. His thoughts returned to an encounter earlier that day, with a young man whom he had turned away from making a sacrifice. The man, barely out of boyhood, had brought a ewe for a sin offering. He had confessed to drinking to excess the week before and making a foolhardy oath in public, calling on God as his witness to an oath he could not keep. His father, the man had explained sullenly, had heard from others of his son's oath and insisted that the young man bring a sin offering to the temple.

Jeshua's solemn eyes had rested on the youth for a long and silent moment. "And what is in your heart, son?"

The youth had met his gaze with a flash of defiance and said, "You sound just like my father. What does it matter what is in my heart? I will be the laughing stock of my friends! They already think I'm a fool since my family makes me sit around on *Shabbat* instead of letting me earn money. And if I made an oath that I can't even remember, what of it? My father burns enough sacrifices for my whole family put together. Surely the Lord can credit some of that stench to me without me having to butcher this sheep."

Jeshua sighed heavily. His sharp rebuke and warning that the youth's unrepented sin would see him cut off from God's family had, sadly, fallen on closed ears. He had sent the young man away, dragging his ewe in tow. Jeshua knew that this young man was not unique, that many in Judah would rather follow the habits of their heathen neighbors than follow God's ways.

He put the incident firmly from his mind, again, as a worn-looking woman entered the courtyard on the arm of a shabbily dressed man. A small bundle bulged across the woman's middle, wrapped in a faded shawl. A tiny, curled hand jerked free from the shawl and then disappeared again. Two trussed birds dangled in the woman's grasp.

"Shalom!" called Jeshua in greeting.

"Shalom!" The couple approached him, and he saw they were older than he had first assumed. The husband placed a protective hand on the bundle slung across his wife's belly.

"After many years of prayer, God has blessed us with a child, a son! We have named him Samuel, 'God hears.' "

"A fitting name indeed for a son so long anticipated," smiled Jeshua, recognizing their reference to Hannah's son, who had later become the prophet Samuel.

"My wife's period of purification is complete—for 40 days she has touched no holy thing nor entered the sanctuary. We have brought two doves as God commands."

Jeshua turned to the mother. "One will serve as your sin offering; its blood will make atonement for you so you may be clean from your flow of blood. The other dove will be your burnt offering; through it you will be rededicated to God and will once again have access to his holiness and blessing."

The woman nodded and handed Jeshua a dove. Jeshua gripped the creature by its feet and walked to the altar of burnt offering. As he untied the dove, it arced upwards and caught his sleeve in its beak, beating the air with frantic wings. Hurriedly, he pinched through its thin neck with his thumbnail and squeezed the bird against the side of the altar so that its blood spurted briefly against the altar stones. The woman now handed him the remaining dove. Jeshua carried the bird up the ramp to the altar of burnt offering. Its pulse throbbed under his fingers. He wrung off its head and placed it on the burning coals, then strode to the edge of the altar to drain its blood. Jeshua then tore open the bird by its wings. He pulled out the bird's intestines and tossed them over the eastern edge of the altar into the ash heap below. Finally, he placed the small carcass on the flames.

Jeshua returned to where the man and his wife stood waiting with respectful stillness. He smiled at them and announced, "It is a burnt offering, a gift of a pleasing aroma to the Lord."

Tears rose in the woman's eyes, and she hastily ducked her head. Jeshua nodded his understanding.

"God is good."

The small bundle let out a squawk, and a tiny fist punched the air. The child's parents smiled proudly, and Jeshua felt his heart twist again when he thought of the young man who had forsaken his parents' faith.

"May God give your son the ears of his namesake, the prophet Samuel, who heard and did not turn from God's counsel," said Jeshua, raising a hand in farewell.

Sacred silhouettes

Mary and Joseph brought baby Jesus along to the temple for Mary's postnatal purification rites when Jesus was 40 days old. In Luke 2:22-24, Mary offered the sacrifice for her own cleansing, and then she presented her firstborn son to God. How she must later have marveled at this astounding truth: the most important sin offering she brought to the temple that day was not the bird in her hand but the baby in her arms!

Romans 8:3 is just one passage in the New Testament that uses the sin offering as a picture of Christ, whom God sent "in the likeness of sinful man to be a *sin offering.*" The sinless Son of God took on human skin, sweat, and blood, and then offered these on the altar of the cross. Because of God's perfect sin offering, Satan, sin, and death have lost their power to harm us.

The law that required the flesh of a high priest's sin offering to be burned "outside the camp" is commented on in Hebrews 13:11,12: "The high priest carries the blood of animals into the Most Holy Place as a sin offering, but the bodies are burned outside the camp. And so Jesus also suffered outside the city gate to make the people holy through his own blood."

Bible reading

The LORD said to Moses: "When a person commits a violation and sins unintentionally in regard to any of the LORD's holy things, he is to bring to the LORD as a penalty a ram from the flock, one without defect and of the proper value in silver, according to the sanctuary shekel. It is a guilt offering." (Leviticus 5:14,15)

Leviticus 5:14–6:7; 7:1-6—The Purpose and Procedure for the Guilt Offering

Leviticus 13:45,46; 14:1-32—Isolating and Cleansing Procedures for Those With a Skin Infection

The guilt offering is the fourth and final blood sacrifice we will examine. The Hebrew term for the guilt offering is *Asham,* which means "trespass." A guilt offering, like a sin offering, was intended to restore the sinner's relationship with God.

It can be a bit confusing to distinguish between a sin offering and a guilt offering. One major difference is that a guilt offering was brought when *repayment* for sin was possible, which is not always the case. And if it was possible to repay the person who was sinned against, the Lord required that the repayment be made.

The animal sacrificed in a guilt offering was always a ram, with no substitute for the poor. The only exception was in the case of a cleansed leper, who brought a male lamb, rather than a ram, as his guilt offering.

As with a private sin offering, the fat was offered to God on the altar and the officiating priest ate the meat in the courtyard.

Three kinds of sins required a guilt offering:

Sin against God's holy things. Examples of this might be bringing an inferior offering to God, eating a sacred offering by mistake, or forgetting a tithe. The priest determined the cost of the worshiper's sin and added to this 20 percent. This reparation money was given to God, through the priest.

Suspected sin against God's holy things. In this case, there was only a suspicion that a sin had been committed. The guilt offering eased a conscience that felt real guilt and feared God's punishment. No repayment or added premium was required, since the sin could not be pinpointed nor its value calculated.

Sin of depriving someone of their property and lying about it under oath (perjury). In this case the guilty person repaid his victim by returning whatever he had stolen, plus a further 20 percent. Only then was the guilty person allowed to bring the ram as his guilt offering.

When an offender's sins directly harmed another person, God required the offender to make amends. This inflated refund taught his people that sin is a debt. (The account of the tax collector Zacchaeus in Luke 19:8 is a New Testament example of restitution in action. Zacchaeus not only vowed to stop his cheating ways, he also paid back with interest what he had stolen!)

However, repayment didn't stop there. A blood sacrifice was also owed to *God*. God was teaching his people that every sin is ultimately a sin against him. He says as much in Numbers 5:6, "When a man or woman wrongs another in any way and so is unfaithful *to the* LORD, that person is guilty." King David, who had taken a man's wife and life, also confessed this truth when he wrote in Psalm 51:4, "Against you, you only, have I sinned and done what is evil in your sight."

The next story requires some explanation. A healed leper was to bring three offerings: two male lambs as guilt and burnt offerings and a ewe for a sin offering. God isn't clear about *why* each offering was necessary: Jewish tradition speculates that skin diseases were punishment for harmful talk or excessive pride (think of Moses' sister Miriam being struck with leprosy after speaking against Moses in Numbers 12:1). According to this tradition, the guilt offering covered the sin of slander that had caused the skin disease; the sin offering covered any sins committed while suffering with the disease (such as reproaching God); and the burnt offering restored the broken relationship with God.

This vignette focuses on the guilt offering offered by Yoni, a leper whose skin disease had healed. While God demands a guilt offering in this situation, he does not require the 20 percent restitution. This is enough to tell us that the leper's guilt is not one that can be calculated in monetary terms. Perhaps the guilt offering was required to cover sin the leper *may* have committed during his period of uncleanness. Ultimately, Yoni brings the guilt offering simply because God says to do so.

The story—Yoni

"Yoni!" bellowed Shlomo's father, hitching up his robe and running out to the courtyard.

Shlomo and Miriam scuttled to the entryway to see what catastrophe could have caused their father to move with such alacrity.

In the courtyard an odd-looking man had wrapped their Aba in a bear hug. After a brief spell of shameless gaping, the children realized what it was that puzzled them about the man's appearance. He had no beard, no eyebrows, and only a dark shadow on his head suggested where his hair had been. The children realized the man had caught them staring, and they ducked their heads and blushed furiously, waiting to be scolded. To their surprise, the man burst into a shout of laughter.

"Natan," he addressed their father. "Those two in the doorway have their beaks open wider than two hungry fledglings!"

"Children!" Their Aba beckoned, and they came shyly forward to meet the stranger. "This is Yoni the tanner, my old friend!"

Natan slapped the hairless man on his back and cried, "Welcome home, my friend! You are healed!"

Yoni grinned and ran a rueful hand over his head, "Healed, and shorn like a spring sheep!"

"Well, my bald friend, you must stay for dinner. Children, run and tell your mother!"

Later, over dinner, Natan leaned forward on his elbow and gently addressed the tanner, "So tell us, friend, what was it like to be *tameh*, unclean, for those many months?"

Yoni's smile faded, and the skin on his forehead contracted where his eyebrows should have been.

"Ah, Natan. It is difficult to find words for that kind of loneliness. I was a pariah to my own wife and children. Barred from the

Lord's temple. For the first time in my life I could not make the Feast of Tabernacles pilgrimage with my family. Instead I . . ." He fumbled for a word, ". . . I *lurked* on the edges of town, my hair uncombed, my clothes torn. Whenever anyone approached me, I had to cover my face and shout, '*Tameh!* Unclean!' "

Yoni was silent for a time, adrift in this recollection. Then he sighed, "I was truly a picture of the curse of sin: dead while yet alive."

He shrugged, and a smile broadened his face. "But, Natan, children: every morning and evening I looked toward Jerusalem. In my mind I could see the smoke rising from the burnt offering for all of Israel. That offering was for me too. It brought me much comfort to be thus rededicated to the Lord, despite being among the living dead."

Natan laid a hand on the tanner's arm. "Forgive me, Yoni, for reminding you of such painful things. You have much to teach me and my children."

Yoni nodded. "It was not an entirely painful experience, Natan. Although I was an outcast, God did not reject me. I knew that I could still serve him with my disease, as a walking, talking picture of the awfulness of sin. And now in his mercy he has healed me."

Shlomo shyly cleared his throat. "What happened when you got better?"

"Well, that is a story!" laughed Yoni. "I was examined outside of town by a priest, who agreed that my skin condition had been healed. The next day the priest and a Levite brought two birds, a stick of cedar, scarlet yarn, hyssop, and a clay pot filled with water." Yoni ticked the items off on fingers that were permanently red and swollen from the rigors of turning animal hides into leather.

"The priest took the first bird and wrung its neck over the pot of spring water, so that its blood flowed into the pot. Then he gathered together the rest in a strange bouquet indeed: hyssop, cedar, yarn, and one frantic, flapping bird, and dipped them into the pot. With this special whisk, he flicked the blood on me, seven times."

"That sounds like what Aba had to do after he buried Grandfather: the cedar, yarn, and hyssop brush was used to sprinkle special water on you, wasn't it, Aba?" blurted Shlomo, bashfulness forgotten.

"Yes. I often thought of that similarity too, young Shlomo," said the tanner. "My status before God was the same as that of a corpse."

A silence pressed on the small group as they considered this. Then Yoni picked up the threads of his story and continued.

"After he had sprinkled me with blood, the priest opened his hands and released the bloodstained bird. It spread its wings and flew upwards until it was swallowed by the clouds. It was as if the disease had been carried away from me; I was brought back from death to life."

"And then you were allowed to go home?" asked Miriam.

"I was allowed to return to town after I had laundered my clothes, shaved all my hair, and bathed, but I could not enter my home. I was not yet ceremonially clean. Seven days later I again washed and shaved. Then I was fit to enter the temple."

"But not your home?" Miriam asked again.

"No. My purification was not complete until I made a pilgrimage to the Holy City on the eighth day. My wife prepared my oil and grain offering, and at the temple I purchased two male lambs and a ewe. A priest led me before the altar and presented one lamb and my olive oil as a guilt offering to the Lord."

"A guilt offering? Why?" asked Shlomo.

"Because it is what the Lord commands in the Torah. But I was glad, Shlomo, for while I was outcast, my conscience had been greatly troubled. I thought that perhaps I had come into God's presence with an inferior offering or I had forgotten a tithe. I wondered if that was why God had allowed my skin disease, in order to bring me to repentance. Yes, the guilt offering is a wonderful blessing for those of us with a bruised and heavy conscience."

Yoni continued, "I laid my hands on the lamb and slaughtered it. But instead of pouring out all of its blood against the altar, the priest reserved some. He dipped his own fingers in the blood of the guilt offering and with it painted the tip of my right ear, the thumb of my right hand, and the toe of my right foot."

Shlomo said, "But Aba taught us that priests are ordained in the same way!"

"That is true," said the tanner. "With each dab of blood I was reminded that the parts of my body that had once belonged to a living corpse now belonged to a purified man. By God's grace I was now fit to hear God's Word, to touch the holy meat of my offerings, and to stand on holy ground. In this ritual God made it clear that my acts of service were now just as acceptable as those of the high priest!"

Yoni let this sink in and then continued, "Not only that, the priest then took the measure of oil and poured it in his palm. He consecrated the oil by sprinkling some before the altar. Then he smeared the remainder on my ear lobe, thumb, and toe, right over the blood of the guilt offering. Finally, he drew the oil across my forehead. I was like a privileged guest anointed by a king! God honored me at his temple, where once I had been an outcast."

"You anoint my head with oil; my cup overflows" (Psalm 23:5b), King David's psalm was rendered by Aba's pleasing tenor. Soon he was joined by the voices of his family and the tanner named Yoni, who no longer belonged to the realm of death but to the realm of life.

Sacred silhouettes

A leper is a vivid picture of the ravages of sin. A leper's body is visibly corrupted, and socially he is like a living corpse. Cleansing only comes through sacrifice and the intervention of the priests.

But what does leprosy have to do with us? David wasn't exaggerating when he said, "Surely I was sinful at birth, sinful from the time my mother conceived me" (Psalm 51:5). We too are sinful from our conception. Even as we grow from zygote to embryo to fetus, we are dead in our sins and we are delivered into this world as spiritual stillborns. We cannot lift our arms to receive the embrace of God's grace. We cannot even part our lips to cry for help. But rather than cast us into the crematorium of hell, Christ intervenes on our behalf as both sacrifice and priest. He wheels our gurneys to the cross and to the font, where he miraculously resuscitates and cleans us. We did not earn or invite or declare our readiness for this intervention. It is ever, only, always a gift of grace!

The prophet Isaiah pictured the coming Messiah as a guilt offering (Isaiah 53:10). By his sacrifice on the cross, Christ paid—in full—our unpaid debt to his Father. In grateful love we eagerly cancel the debts of those who have wronged us, fully and freely forgiving, just as Christ forgave us.

13 THE PASSOVER

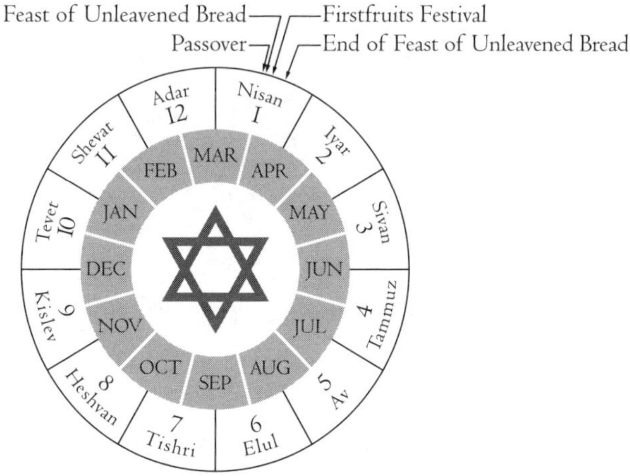

Bible reading

"These are the LORD's appointed feasts, the sacred assemblies you are to proclaim at their appointed times: The LORD's Passover begins at twilight on the fourteenth day of the first month. On the fifteenth day of that month the LORD's Feast of Unleavened Bread begins; for seven days you must eat bread made without yeast. On the first day hold a sacred assembly and do no regular work. For seven days present an offering made to the LORD by fire. And on the seventh day hold a sacred assembly and do no regular work." (Leviticus 23:4-8)

"After the LORD brings you into the land of the Canaanites and gives it to you, as he promised on oath to you and your forefathers, you are to give over to the LORD the first offspring of every womb. All the firstborn males of your livestock belong to the LORD. Redeem with a lamb every firstborn donkey, but if you do not redeem it, break its neck. Redeem every firstborn among your sons.

"In days to come, when your son asks you, 'What does this mean?' say to him, 'With a mighty hand the LORD brought us out of Egypt, out of

the land of slavery. When Pharaoh stubbornly refused to let us go, the LORD killed every firstborn in Egypt, both man and animal. This is why I sacrifice to the LORD the first male offspring of every womb and redeem each of my firstborn sons.' And it will be like a sign on your hand and a symbol on your forehead that the LORD brought us out of Egypt with his mighty hand." (Exodus 13:11-16)

Leviticus 23:4-8; Numbers 28:16-25—The Passover and Feast of Unleavened Bread
Leviticus 23:9-14—Festival of Firstfruits
Exodus 12—The First Passover in Egypt
Numbers 9:1-14—The Second Passover in the Desert of Sinai
Exodus 13:11-16—Redemption of the Firstborn
Numbers 3:44-51—Redemption Price

The Passover, or *Pesach*, was the first pilgrimage festival of the Israelite *church* year. It took place on the 14th of *Abib* (our March/April). The Passover commemorated God's rescue of Israel from Egypt. An unblemished lamb or goat was selected, slaughtered, roasted whole, and eaten with unleavened bread and bitter herbs.

The Passover was intertwined with two other festivals, the Feast of Unleavened Bread and the Festival of Firstfruits. Some pilgrims remained in Jerusalem for the following days:

Abib 14: Passover began at sundown. Homes were yeast free. Each family shared a meal of a sacrificial lamb and unleavened bread, while recounting their deliverance from Egypt.

Abib 15: Passover ended at sundown, and the weeklong Feast of Unleavened Bread began. Homes remained yeast free for the next seven days. Representatives of the family had to be present at the sanctuary only on the first day of the feast (*Abib* 16).

Abib 17: The Festival of Firstfruits took place, and the Israelites "waved," or presented, the first sheaf of their spring barley harvest to God in thanksgiving and to publicly acknowledge that their daily bread came from him. This day was pivotal to the Israelites, since they were not allowed to eat any new grain before they had dedicated their first-ripe produce to God.

Abib 21: The Feast of Unleavened Bread concluded, and pilgrims returned home.

The Passover was so important that those who missed it for legitimate reasons were to celebrate it a month later. Anyone who failed to celebrate the Passover was to be cut off from his people (Numbers 9:9-13).

Do you remember the first Passover in Egypt? Twilight arrived with a mass slaughtering of year-old lambs that had been specially selected and cared for during the previous five days. Shivers of apprehension should have run up the spines of the Egyptians as the Israelites painted their doorways using bunches of hyssop dipped in lamb's blood. The Israelites ate in haste, wearing their traveling clothes. At midnight, God's destroying angel struck the firstborn in Egypt but passed over the houses of the Israelites. In the dark hours of the morning, a loud wailing shook Egypt, and Pharaoh gasped, "Go!" The Israelites wrapped up their remaining unleavened dough in bundles of clothing and baked and ate it en route. The Lord himself kept vigil that night so the Israelites could safely leave Egypt. In response, the Israelites were to keep vigil on this night to honor the Lord for generations to come (Exodus 12:42).

How carefully God planned that last dinner in Egypt, by which he provided his people with a picture of his salvation plan! God's Passover menu included unleavened bread and roasted lamb. The bread without yeast was both practical and symbolic. Since the Israelites left Egypt in haste, like a businessman hurrying to catch the last bus home, they didn't have time to wait for yeasted dough to rise before baking it. But God also used the unleavened bread to impress on his people that just as no yeast "contaminated" their bread that night, so no sin was to contaminate their lips, hands, or hearts.

Of course that was impossible. It was one thing to bake bread without yeast but quite another to go a whole evening, much less a lifetime, without, for example, snubbing a sibling or provoking a parent. That flat piece of unleavened bread may as well have been a miniature stone tablet of the Ten Commandments. It symbolized a standard that the Israelites could only fail to meet.

Enter the roasted lamb as the main course on God's Passover menu! This was the lamb whose blood dripped from the doorframes of Israelite homes. That scarlet strip of blood was a firebreak beyond which God's anger would not burn. The blood of the lamb kept the destroying angel from crossing the threshold of the Israelite homes and striking dead the firstborn sons.

Each time the Israelites ate the Passover meal, they were reminded of God's desire for them to be pure and of God's plan to save them from their impurity through the blood of a substitute.

The story—Shlomo and his family celebrate the Passover

Preparations for Passover began in mid-February, a whole six weeks before the festival. The elders of Hebron set up a table in the central market near the city gates. Aba took along Shlomo to contribute a half shekel to the temple treasury (Exodus 30:11-16).

"What will the elders do with our money, Aba?" asked Shlomo.

"They will appoint someone to take the money to the temple treasurers in Jerusalem. The money will be used throughout the coming year to purchase animals for the public offerings, like the morning and evening sacrifices and the festival sacrifices."

A few days before their annual *Pesach* pilgrimage, Shlomo observed that his mother bore an increasing resemblance to a summer dust storm, whirling from one room to the other and gathering into her fervent vortex whatever and whoever wasn't fastened down or otherwise occupied.

One afternoon, eager to escape another task, Shlomo sought the company of his Aba. His father had spent the morning in the field, harvesting the first ripe sheaves of barley. He was now sitting on a stone in the courtyard, face upturned to the warm spring sunshine and conveniently out of the line of vision from the front door. Beyond the tangle of blind alleys and dense housing, the hills were a constellation of new lambs and wildflowers.

"Aba, tell me what is happening in Jerusalem to prepare for *Pesach*."

His father closed his eyes, the better to conjure up a vision for Shlomo.

"Ah, the Holy City in the weeks before the Passover: right now it is a hive of activity. Merchants with voices like broken *shofars,* rams' horns, are vying for the best spaces in the city market. Innkeepers are chasing cobwebs from their empty rooms, anticipating crowds of weary wayfarers. Men from the temple have been delegated to fill potholes in the roads and slather whitewash on overgrown graves so that no ritually clean pilgrim will be accidentally defiled by contact with an old grave. In a few weeks, pilgrims from all over the country will raise great clouds of dust on those roads as they converge on Jerusalem and Solomon's temple for *Pesach,* the festival of freedom!"

"And we will be among them!" said Shlomo, thrilled at his father's imagery.

"Yes, indeed," said his father, adding dryly, "assuming we survive your Ima's preparations."

One week later, on the 14th day of *Abib,* Shlomo, Miriam, their Ima and Aba, and a large and boisterous crowd of fellow pilgrims entered Jerusalem, many leading lambs and laden with bedding, clay pots, and dishes. Shlomo caught snatches of conversations in strange dialects and accents. Miriam tugged at the rope that was tied to their lamb. Shlomo noticed his Ima directing sidelong glances at Miriam. Despite their parents' warnings, his little sister had become quite fond of the creature during the week they had cared for it. Shlomo shrugged and allowed the sea of elbows and legs to carry him along while he imagined that he was a child of the exodus, one of two million jostling Israelites who had just crossed the Red Sea into freedom.

Natan had arranged for the family to stay with Lev, a distant cousin who lived in the Lower City. Shlomo and Miriam were dusty and tired by the time Cousin Lev called a greeting from his doorway. They were quickly surrounded by a small band of children of varying ages.

"Shalom, Natan!" Cousin Lev clapped Shlomo's father heartily on the back. "Welcome to my home and my little tribe—I cannot keep them straight myself, so we will wait until later to make formal introductions. I have just started the fire so that it will be ready to roast our lamb tonight. But now you must wash and slake your thirst. We will leave the women to sweep up any stray yeast and prepare *matzot,* unleavened bread, while we men head to the temple to make the Passover offering."

Shlomo and his oldest cousin beamed to be thus labeled, and soon the four of them were back in the press of pilgrims proceeding to the temple, each party carrying a lamb. As the crowd shuffled up the sloping road to the temple gates, the air vibrated with blasts from the Levites' *shofars* and silver trumpets and with the raised voices of Levites and pilgrims in *Hallel,* praise, psalms.[11] Punctuating the music was the frantic bleating of anxious animals. On top of the hill, Shlomo could see a boiling black shaft of smoke. The wind gusted, slapping him with the acrid stench of whole animals being burned. Above the coiling column of smoke, kites and buzzards drew lazy circles across the high blue sky. Shlomo squeezed his Aba's hand, filled with excitement and dread.

"Will we see the high priest, Aba?" he yelled over the din.

"He will be there, son. Here, it is our turn now. You will see for yourself."

The East Gate of the courtyard groaned open, disgorging pilgrims carrying the carcasses of their Passover lambs. The Levite gatekeepers ushered in the next group. Shlomo's eyes widened at the sight in the temple courtyard. All along the courtyard up to the altar of burnt offering stood two rows of priests, their white linens stained with wet, red blooms. Every priest held a bowl. As each pilgrim slaughtered his lamb, a priest would catch the blood in his bowl and pass the filled bowl from priest to priest, up to the altar. The priest nearest the altar jerked the blood against the base of the altar. In the midst of this activity, the Levites sang, *"Hallelu,* O you servants of Jehovah." The people echoed, *"Hallelujah!* Praise the LORD!" (see Psalm 113).

Shlomo's foot slipped in something wet. His father reached down to steady him, then knelt with the lamb, which trembled at the tang of blood that soaked the stones underfoot. Shlomo squeezed his eyes shut as his father drew out a knife. When he opened them again, the bowl of blood was traveling hand to hand toward the altar. Shlomo craned his neck and saw the high priest,

---

[11]According to later Jewish liturgical usage, Psalms 113–118 were sung during the great feasts like Passover (John Brug, *A Commentary on Psalms 1–72,* p. 28).

robes as brilliant as a bird's feathers, atop the altar, laying pieces of the sacrifices on the fire. Fat crackled. Smoke poured into the sky. Thick flakes of ash settled on the crowd. A priest took their lamb and began to skin the carcass.

Finally the gates opened, and Shlomo staggered out into the late afternoon sun and sucked in a lungful of clean air. For the first time in his life, Shlomo had a tangible understanding of what his Aba had tried so hard to convey: that without blood you cannot approach God.

When they reached Cousin Lev's house, the women were busy preparing bitter herbs and wrapping fresh unleavened bread in towels to keep them warm. Miriam looked up from her task, and her mouth quivered when she saw what was left of her lamb. Ima gave Miriam's shoulder a brisk pat as Lev and his oldest sons maneuvered the lamb carcass onto a spit. Soon the courtyard was filled with a rich aroma of roast meat. The children hovered nearby, mouths watering with anticipation. Eventually even Miriam joined in the good-natured bragging about who would eat the most. As Lev turned the spit, his youngest son asked, eyes alight with curiosity, "Aba, why is this night different from all other nights?"

"Tonight we will eat the Passover lamb, roasted whole with bones unbroken, as God commands. When we eat this lamb, we recall the blood of the lamb that our forefathers painted on their doorposts in Egypt. When God bent his anger on Egypt because of Pharaoh's hard heart, he passed over every house with the sign of blood." Cousin Lev looked up from the fire and grinned. "I trust you children are all ravenous so that no meat will remain until morning?" The children assented with a loud whoop, and Lev continued. "Tonight no leavened food will be eaten, and your mothers have made certain that no yeast is within our home. This is to remember our forefathers who fled from Pharaoh with no time for their bread to rise. We will eat *maror*, bitter herbs, to recall the bitter time of slavery in Egypt and how God broke the bars of our yoke and enabled us to walk with our heads held high."

Aba laid a hand on Shlomo's shoulder. "Don't forget, Lev, how we redeemed our firstborn sons, as the Lord commanded during the exodus. More than a week's wages we paid to the priests for our sons when they were a month old."

"Why, Aba?" asked Shlomo, though he had heard the story many times.

"God took the lives of the firstborn of every Egyptian family, but he spared the Israelite children. Our firstborn sons and male livestock therefore belong to God, and we buy you back in order to always recall how 'the LORD brought you out of [Egypt] with a mighty hand' " (Exodus 13:3).

"And we will continue to remember our deliverance tomorrow and for the rest of the week," Lev added. He looked up from his task, and Shlomo could see the light of the coals glittering in his eyes. "For tomorrow night, on the 15th of *Abib*, we will begin our celebration of the Feast of Unleavened Bread. For seven days we will not eat any food with yeast. On the first and last days of the week, we will do no work in our fields or businesses. These are holy days during which we will bring our offerings to the temple."

Natan said, "We have brought our firstfruits from our barley fields, is that not so, Shlomo? This week during the Feast of Unleavened Bread, we will take our first sheaf of ripe barley to the temple, along with our fellow farmers. The high priest himself will elevate the first sheaves and present them to God on behalf of our nation."

"And only after we have given God this first sample of the new harvest will God's people eat any of the grain. In this way we remember that our daily bread comes from God!" concluded Lev.

He prodded the meat on the spit with a forefinger. "But now our lamb is ready. It is time to share the Passover Feast!"

The courtyard cleared in a hurry. Shlomo touched his father's sleeve and nodded toward the rooftop. A full moon was rising. They lingered until the last tinge of blood had drained from its bowl and a cold, liquid light spilled over Jerusalem. Then together they turned and entered the house to celebrate the Passover.

Sacred silhouettes

The first Lord's Supper took place in an upstairs room in Jerusalem, on the night of the Passover (Mark 14:12). How fitting! As Jesus and his disciples shared unleavened bread, they would have recalled—along with every devout Jew since ancient times—how the Passover bread had strengthened their forefathers for the journey to Canaan. But now Jesus offered his friends a new meal—his own body—to sustain them on their journey to the *heavenly* promised land! And as Jesus and his followers ate the Passover lamb, they would have recalled—as they had since childhood—the blood-trimmed doorframes in ancient Egypt. But now Jesus offered them *his* blood: blood that would, the very next day, be painted on the wood of the cross, the doorframe that stood between God's destroying anger and the whole world![12]

When we partake of the bread and wine of Communion, we are not eating and drinking symbols. We receive exactly what Jesus said: the real body and blood of Christ. Those who believe what God promises about this heavenly meal also enjoy what it imparts: real salvation, real strength, real comfort. It's a real miracle!

The Passover and Feast of Unleavened Bread were preceded by a flurry of activity as Jewish homes were scoured and swept for any errant crumbs of yeast. First Corinthians 5:7,8 refers to this custom when it says, "Get rid of the old yeast [of malice and wickedness] that you may be a new batch without yeast—as you really are. For Christ, our Passover lamb, has been sacrificed."

The Passover lamb was a shadow of Jesus in several ways: it was familiar, male, unblemished, and slaughtered. John 19:36 adds a further similarity. Just as the lamb was to be roasted without its bones being broken, so Jesus' bones were not broken, unlike the bones of the two thieves with whom he was crucified.

Finally, it is hard not to notice with what swift mercy the priests sacrificed the Passover lambs. Yet how brutal they were with the Lamb of God: binding, mocking, and beating him before demanding an agonizing crucifixion! And though the Son of God could have dismounted that cross in a heartbeat, he did not, because his heart beat for us!

---

[12]William Cwirla, *Five Sermons on the Sacraments*, http://blog.higherthings.org/wcwirla/The%20Sermonator/sermons%20on%20the%20sacraments.html

FEAST OF WEEKS/PENTECOST 14

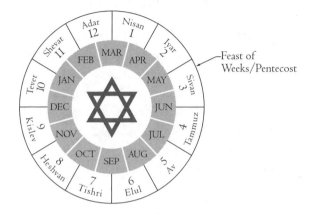

Feast of Weeks/Pentecost

Bible reading

"On the day of firstfruits, when you present to the LORD an offering of new grain during the Feast of Weeks, hold a sacred assembly and do no regular work. Present a burnt offering of two young bulls, one ram and seven male lambs a year old as an aroma pleasing to the LORD. With each bull there is to be a grain offering of three-tenths of an ephah of fine flour mixed with oil; with the ram, two-tenths; and with each of the seven lambs, one-tenth. Include one male goat to make atonement for you. Prepare these together with their drink offerings, in addition to the regular burnt offering and its grain offering. Be sure the animals are without defect." (Numbers 28:26-31)

Leviticus 23:15-22; Exodus 23:16a; 34:22a; Numbers 28:26-31; Deuteronomy 16:9-12; Acts 2:1-4—The Feast of Weeks

The Feast of Weeks (also called the Feast of Harvest), or *Shavuot*, was the second pilgrim festival in the Jewish church calendar. The Feast of Weeks took place in *Sivan* (our May/June), 50 days after the Festival of Firstfruits, which was two days after the Passover.

The Feast of Weeks was a day of rest, marking the ritual end of the wheat harvest. We can think of it as an Old Testament Thanksgiving celebration. In later Judaism it came to commemorate another event that took place 50 days after the first Passover and the liberation of the Israelites from Egypt: God's giving of the Law at Mount Sinai.

On the Feast of Weeks, God commanded the Israelites to bring to the temple as the firstfruits from their harvest two loaves of wheat bread made with yeast. This bread was leavened, unlike the grain offerings that were burnt on the altar. According to Jewish tradition, farmers from around Jerusalem filled their baskets with food on Pentecost morning. They fell in step behind a flute player, who led them up the temple mount as they sang the songs of ascents (Psalms 120–136).

The king himself placed a basket of food on his shoulder and led the people into the temple courts as the Levites sang Psalm 30, a song that David had written for the temple dedication. These offerings were presented together with a burnt offering of seven lambs, two rams, and one bull; a sin offering of a male goat; and a fellowship offering of two male lambs. The meat of the fellowship offering and the loaves of leavened bread were eaten by the priests on duty.

God's people also participated in this day by leaving the edges of their fields unreaped and the fallen stalks of grain on the ground so that the poor could gather them (Leviticus 23:22). Just as God provided for the priests through the grain and fellowship offerings, so he also cared for the poor and alien in Israel with the gleanings of the harvest. Imagine faithful Ruth tirelessly stooping and filling her basket with the fallen stalks from Boaz' field to provide for herself and her widowed mother-in-law, Naomi. How thankful she must have been for such legislation and for a God-fearing man like Boaz who observed this ritual.

The story—The meaning and value of the Feast of Weeks

Shlomo's Ima clucked her tongue with dismay as she surveyed his bare ankles and, high above them, the hem of his robe. During the seven weeks of harvest that followed the Passover, Shlomo had grown as fast as the spring barley, faster perhaps; and Ima had lengthened his robe as far as the hem would allow. His arms were brown and sinewy from hours spent handling the oxen and plow and swinging a scythe in the fields with his Aba. Now it was *Sivan,* and the green carpet of wheat that had replaced the spring barley harvest had ripened into golden sheaves.

In *Sivan,* 50 days after the Passover celebration, another pilgrimage festival would take place: *Shavuot,* the Feast of Weeks. Despite this festival falling at a time when farmers were wedded to their fields from sunrise until dark, God had commanded his people to again gather their harvest offerings and set out for Jerusalem.

Shlomo's Aba was in the middle of his annual *Shavuot* speech: an inventory of thanksgiving aimed at whoever would listen. He had extolled the growing wheat, the weather, his children and wife. Now he had moved on to his favorite subject: the ancient stories of Moses and the exodus. His voice rose, and his arms pumped with excitement. "Picture it, children: God shakes Mount Sinai with thunder and lightning. Smoke billows. A trumpet blares with a sound like none on earth. And into that chaos climbs a gray-headed Moses. He disappears into the smoke and fire that surrounds God. And when he finally descends, he carries two tablets of stone on which God's finger has carved the commandments!"

Miriam hung on his every word, but Shlomo was aware of a rising irritation that he batted down like a troublesome fly. Shlomo ducked away from his Ima's fussing hands and sought a quiet spot under the courtyard fig tree. His father intended to take Shlomo to Jerusalem in a week for *Shavuot,* the spring harvest festival. The Feast of Weeks was a day of rest that celebrated the wheat harvest, and pilgrims were to bring fresh loaves of leavened bread made with the new wheat as firstfruits offerings to the Lord. The loaves would be presented to the Lord, along with many blood sacrifices. Festive pilgrims would stream into Jerusalem, though not as many as for Passover. In fact, many from Shlomo's own circle of friends did not plan to go with their fathers.

"Shlomo." His father's voice interrupted his reverie. Aba stood before Shlomo, his eyes crinkled with concern. "You have something on your mind, yes? Jeshua says you have not visited him of late. Perhaps you could share your burden with me."

Shlomo considered holding his tongue. He was sometimes ashamed of his growing impatience with his parents, but he was, after all, not so much a child anymore. Their ways were fine, but they did not have to be his ways. It embarrassed him to recall how the recent Passover sacrifices had left him breathless with awe. When he had returned from the pilgrimage and shared his experience with his older friends, they had shrugged away his amazement on bored shoulders. Now he realized that he had acted just as babyish as his little sister, Miriam.

Shlomo cleared his throat. "Some of my friends are not making the pilgrimage this year. Their fathers say it is too difficult to leave the wheat crop at harvesttime." He stopped for a moment, then blundered on. "I thought it would be good for me to stay home too. And look after the fields," he finished weakly.

Twin spots of color surfaced on Natan's cheeks, and Shlomo braced himself for a scolding. He was not disappointed.

"Tell me, son, why should we not trust God to protect our harvest in our absence? Is it not the Lord who gives showers of rain and plants of the field to everyone? Does he not say to us in the psalms, 'Open wide your mouth and I will fill it' (Psalm 81:10b)? What do your wise friends say to that? Pah! Perhaps they only open wide their mouths so that they can fill the air with their fine opinions!"

Shlomo's hands balled into fists, but he didn't speak. A silence yawned between the boy and his father that Natan finally, gently, broke.

"Shlomo, my son, forgive me. I know that you are only speaking out of a young man's desire to know the right way of things. There are many of God's people who neglect the right way, God's way, because it seems too hard. Many of our brothers to the north prefer idols of goats and calves—they want to be like the peoples of the world who serve wood and stone! Even here in Judah there are plenty who confess faith with their mouths but have forgotten how to trust God with their hearts, let alone their harvests." He twitched his chin at the fields beyond their walls. "How many have remembered to leave the corners of their fields unreaped and the fallen stalks of grain on the ground for the poor to gather so that they too are provided for, so that even the poor can observe the pilgrimage of thanksgiving?"

Natan sighed gustily. "Each day I pray that you and your sister do not neglect God's law. As Moses told the people of Israel, it is no empty word for us. It is our life. That is why we study the Torah, to better understand that God's law is a yoke he places on us in love. It guards us from sin and sets us apart as God's people. It reminds us of the two sides of his face: his justice and his mercy. God forbid we take either one for granted."

Shlomo's Aba stared at the ground. "But perhaps I have not taught you as I should. You are at an age, Shlomo, where you will have to choose whom you will serve." A pause. Then, quietly, "But as for me and my house, we will serve the Lord."

An imaginary line had been drawn in the dust. It was the challenge for which Shlomo had been half-waiting, his chance to use the arguments he had heard from his friends and practiced in his head: Does God really expect us to . . . ? Perhaps what God *meant* was . . . Our own neighbors don't . . . and on and on. He had expected his father to rage and lecture. Yet when the challenge came, so devoid of hostility, Shlomo felt only a sudden, hot flood of shame.

Shlomo laid a hand, awkwardly, over his father's hand, feeling its dear, familiar network of thick veins and calluses.

"Aba," he said, "you talk to us about God when we sit at home, as we work in the fields, and as we walk along. You have fixed those words in our hearts. You have taught us, Aba."

His father did not look at him. But a moment later he turned up his palm and squeezed Shlomo's fingers tightly in his own.

Sacred silhouettes

Pentecost is the Greek name for the Feast of Weeks. *Pentecost* means "fiftieth" and refers to the 50 days in the Jewish year between the Festival of Firstfruits and the Feast of Weeks. Pentecost is much more familiar to us New Testament Christians since it marks the close of our Easter season.

In Acts chapter 2 we hear how Jerusalem was filled with "God-fearing Jews from every nation under heaven" who were observing the Feast of Weeks, or Pentecost, by bringing their freewill offerings to the temple. But it was to be no ordinary harvest celebration. God had bigger plans in mind! He poured out his Holy Spirit on Jesus' disciples, and they wasted no time in witnessing to the crowds in the streets. A different harvest was gathered that day: three thousand people came to faith and were baptized.

Like a lump of dough that balloons with a pinch of yeast, God's church grew quickly from its humble beginning. Perhaps this was the picture God had in mind when he legislated that the loaves of bread on Pentecost were to have yeast, even though grain offerings were normally yeast free.

Have you noticed how many of the festivals that God decreed corresponded to the two harvests in Israel? Passover to Pentecost focused on the culmination of the grain harvest, while the Feast of Trumpets to the Feast of Tabernacles focused on the culmination of the grape and olive harvest.

God used the natural rhythms of the agricultural year to foreshadow certain New Testament truths. Consider the spring festivals of Passover, Firstfruits, and the Feast of Weeks. God used these festivals to point ahead to Christ's first coming. Let's see how:

1. During the celebration of the Passover and Feast of Unleavened Bread, Jesus instituted the Lord's Supper and died on the cross.

2. On the day of the Festival of Firstfruits, Jesus rose from the dead—the firstfruits of all believers who will share in his resurrection by faith (1 Corinthians 15:20-23).

3. Fifty days later came the harvest celebration of the Feast of Weeks. The disciples were filled with the Holy Spirit; thus fortified, they witnessed to the pilgrims and harvested three thousand souls.

The following chart highlights the relationship between the Old Testament spring festivals and events in the New Testament. The dates on the slide indicate the days in *Abib* on which the events occurred (e.g., Passover occurred on the 14th day of *Abib*).

Old Testament		New Testament
The Passover begins at sundown. The family joins in eating the Passover meal of the sacrificial lamb.	Thursday 14th	**Jesus institutes the Lord's Supper while celebrating the Passover.** "Christ, our Passover lamb, has been sacrificed." (I Corinthians 5:7)
The Passover ends at sundown. The Feast of Unleavened Bread begins. This feast shows the results of the Passover. God's people have been cleansed and saved by the blood of the lamb. Sin, which is symbolized by yeast, has been removed from the believer's life.	Friday 15th	**Jesus is sacrificed and dies shortly before 3 o'clock. He is laid in the tomb before sundown.** "Get rid of the old yeast that you may be a new batch without yeast—as you really are. For Christ, our Passover lamb, has been sacrificed." (I Corinthians 5:7)
Sabbath, the day of rest.	Saturday 16th	**Jesus' body lies in the tomb.**
The firstfruits. Israel offers the best of its crop to the Lord, thanking him for his blessings past and future.	Sunday 17th	**Jesus rises from the dead.** "Christ has indeed been raised from the dead, the firstfruits of those who have fallen asleep." (I Corinthians 15:20)

An organized family member will mark special days on the family's calendar a year ahead of time in order to mentally note and prepare for those upcoming events. In a much grander fashion, this is what God did with the Jewish church calendar. More than a millennium before Jesus came to fulfill the Old Testament ceremonies, God penciled those rituals into the Jewish calendar. They were shadows of what was to come. When we flip the pages to the New Testament, we see that those events are fulfilled and circled in red—the red of Jesus' blood. Truly, there are no accidents in God's calendar!

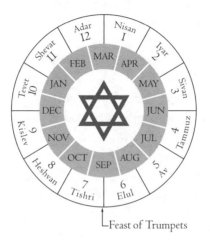

└─Feast of Trumpets

Bible reading

"On the first day of the seventh month hold a sacred assembly and do no regular work. It is a day for you to sound the trumpets. As an aroma pleasing to the LORD, prepare a burnt offering of one young bull, one ram and seven male lambs a year old, all without defect. With the bull prepare a grain offering of three-tenths of an ephah of fine flour mixed with oil; with the ram, two-tenths; and with each of the seven lambs, one-tenth. Include one male goat as a sin offering to make atonement for you. These are in addition to the monthly and daily burnt offerings with their grain offerings and drink offerings as specified. They are offerings made to the LORD by fire—a pleasing aroma." (Numbers 29:1-6)

Leviticus 23:23-25; Numbers 29:1-6—Feast of Trumpets
Nehemiah 8:1-12—Observation of the Feast of Trumpets After the Babylonian Captivity

The Feast of Trumpets, or *Rosh Hashanah*, was celebrated on the first day of *Tishri. Tishri* I was the civil New Year's Day and the beginning of a new harvest cycle. You may recall that *Tishri* was also the seventh and holiest month of the Jewish church year. The Feast of Trumpets was the prologue to a month that also observed the solemn Day of Atonement on *Tishri* 10 and, at the blossoming of the full moon, the joyous Feast of Tabernacles on *Tishri* 15.

Trumpets and rams' horns sounded all day to herald the New Year and to proclaim God's wondrous works. The blast of horns also called the nation to repentance in preparation for the Day of Atonement. In present-day celebrations of *Rosh Hashanah*, devout Jews walk to a river and empty their pockets into the flowing waters, symbolically casting off their sins just as God "hurl[s] all our iniquities into the depths of the sea" (Micah 7:19).

Rosh Hashanah was a day of rest. No servile work was done. The day opened and closed with the regular burnt offerings but also included New Moon offerings: a sin offering of a goat and festive burnt offerings of a young bull, a ram, and seven male lambs.

Although the solemn Day of Atonement was just around the corner, the Feast of Trumpets was a day of joy, not of gloom. Scripture records a particularly poignant Feast of Trumpets in Nehemiah 8:1-12. In this account, the Jewish captives had returned from Babylon. From the Holy City's rubble, the walls of Jerusalem had been newly rebuilt. After years of spiritual decline, war, and captivity, the ceremonies and rituals recorded in Leviticus had been terribly neglected, shockingly forgotten. When *Tishri*, the holy seventh month arrived, Ezra the priest fetched the Torah and from daybreak until noon read it aloud before a large assembly of Israelites. The people wept as they listened to the words of the Law and realized their sins. But Ezra urged them to dry their tears and instead to celebrate, to feast and drink, and to share their abundance with the poor.

The story—Usher in the new year

The land of Judah had been hard-baked by the relentless heat and sun of summer. Small fissures in the earth gaped like parched lips. The grains of a fertile spring were long stored. Grapes and olives had bulged and ripened and been gathered. Now was a time of waiting, watching for the autumn rain to lay down the dust, soften the land, and prepare it for new birth. Breakfast dangled from dusty branches: children foraged for ruby-red pomegranates, broke them open, and plundered the white pith for their sweet jewels. Round figs in hues of copper, bronze, and dark purple were eaten out of hand—their thin, tender skin peeled back from the stem to expose the flesh. On the eve of *Tishri*, a scorched and summer-weary Judah stretched under a moonless sky; only a thin pink line of dawn pushed up the dark.

Somewhere, a boy named Shlomo still slept: a boy who had turned a corner on childhood and who had, by God's grace, chosen well whom he would serve.

Near him stood a father named Natan, who gazed at his son's sleeping face with an upwelling of love for this boy who had begun a cycle of rebellion and repentance that would last a lifetime.

Somewhere a young priest named Jeshua anticipated the new day on his knees, thanking God for guiding him through the joys, pains, and privileges of his first year of ministry among God's people.

And on the temple mount, a high priest named Johanan solemnly donned his kingly regalia, prepared for a day of ritual and rejoicing in a new year of God's grace. Johanan slowly wound his waistband around his robe, listening intently to the voices that floated up from the temple courtyard, as the Levites practiced the Song of Asaph:

> "Sing for joy to God our strength;
> shout aloud to the God of Jacob!
> Sound the ram's horn at the New Moon.
> He says, "I removed the burden from their shoulders;
> Their hands were set free from the basket.
> In your distress you called and I rescued you. . . .
> Listen to me, O Israel!" (Psalm 81:1,3a,6,7a,8b)

Perhaps, thought Johanan, this would be the year the Messiah would answer their call for rescue from sin, rising up to say, "Here I am, I have come—it is written about me in the scroll" (Psalm 40:7). Even as a deep sigh of longing escaped Johanan, he realized he was smiling. Today the Israelites would rejoice over God's mighty acts. Today they would honor God, who still removed "the burden from their shoulders"—no more the yoke of slavery but the yoke of sin.

Johanan hesitated at his chamber door. He traced his finger over the 12 names engraved on the large onyx stones fastened to his shoulder pieces. These were the 12 tribes he represented, the nation he loved. Yet how much more God loved them! Because of God's great love, his people were not destroyed. Soon, on the Day of Atonement, Johanan would pass behind the veil into the Most Holy Place. A scapegoat would carry away the burden of their sin. Johanan's preparations for that most sacred day had already begun. A customary prickle ran over his skin at the thought of standing in God's presence, as a man both inadequate and privileged beyond compare.

Johanan gathered his robes about him and hurried down to the temple courtyard.

From the temple parapets a cry rang out, "The sky is lit as far as Hebron!"

With a groan, the great gates of the temple swung open.

In the courtyard a lamb quietly gave up its blood for the morning burnt offering.

A sonorous swell of rams' horns and the peal of silver trumpets shook Jerusalem from its sleep.

And in a single voice, the Levitical choir chanted,

> *"Come, let us sing for joy to the LORD;*
> *let us shout aloud to the Rock of our salvation.*
> *. . . for he is our God*
> *and we are the people of his pasture,*
> *the flock under his care."* (Psalm 95:1,7)

Sacred silhouettes

We explored in the previous chapter how the spring festivals of Passover, the Festival of Firstfruits, and Pentecost foreshadowed Christ's *first* coming.

The fall festivals—the Feast of Trumpets, the Day of Atonement, and the Feast of Tabernacles—are similar road signs, pointing to Christ's *second* coming on judgment day. Let's see how:

During the Feast of Trumpets, horns and trumpets ushered in the holy seventh month. In the same way, when the Last Day arrives, "the trumpet will sound, the dead will be raised" (1 Corinthians 15:52).

The Day of Atonement pictured the guilt of the Israelite nation being cleansed and removed by innocent substitutes (see chapters 1 and 2). Because of that blood, God, in his mercy, did not punish the people for their sins. Similarly, on judgment day, God will publically declare believers to be not guilty. All our sins were charged to the account of his innocent Son, who became "sin for us, so that in him we might become the righteousness of God" (2 Corinthians 5:21).

The Feast of Tabernacles commemorated the Israelites' march to the Promised Land, acknowledged God's providence, and celebrated the fruit harvest (see chapter 4). It foreshadowed our march to heaven under God's guidance and the final harvest of souls on judgment day. Revelation 7:9,10 pictures God's people, gathered from all corners of the world, surrounding God's throne with palm branches in hand. Their combined voices are an echo of the Feast of Tabernacles, when the Israelites marched before God's altar, shaking bouquets of palm branches and willow.

What a tapestry God has woven for those with eyes of faith! And how privileged we are to see it! What Jesus said privately to his disciples, he also says to us: "Blessed are the eyes that see what you see. For I tell you that many prophets and kings wanted to see what you see but did not see it, and to hear what you hear but did not hear it" (Luke 10:23,24).

From eternity God created the pattern of salvation. In the Garden of Eden he secured his tapestry's base strings: one born of a woman would destroy the devil's work. Over and under these strings God wove a pattern of redemption with ever-increasing detail. What rich and vibrant colors are found in the laws of Leviticus! A weaver works his yarn forwards and backwards across his loom. In the same way God interwove the Old and New Testaments. They meet in the shape of Christ's cross and empty tomb.

In heaven we will see the full and glorious tapestry of salvation with our own eyes, just as Job anticipated: "In my flesh I will see God; I myself will see him with my own eyes—I, and not another. How my heart yearns within me!" (Job 19:26b,27).